PRAISE FOR T.J. MARCHITELLI

T.J. Marchitelli's *What NOT to Do When Your Husband Dies* is a necessary read for anyone. Grief can manifest from a number of different situations - lose of a job, ending a marriage, a loved one passing - and *What NOT to do* is full of practical advice on how to manage the lifelong process. Marchitelli gently guides us through processing & understanding grief through her own personal experience. I can't recommend a better guide for everyone to keep on their bookcase for when grief comes for a visit, as it will.

— BRANDEE MELCHER, AUTHOR OF, *THE BREAK: REDISCOVERING OUR INNER KNOWING*

A powerful guide for the newly bereaved. Mindfulness and meditation can be essential tools to avoid many of the pitfalls possible while one's mind is traumatized by grief. What is powerfully new and helpful here is the understanding of the neuroscience behind the grief process. Marchitelli offers a brave, heartfelt account of personal loss and lessons learned. Highly recommended.

— MIMI RICH, MARRIAGE AND FAMILY THERAPIST

A compelling read. This book could be a lifeboat for people dealing with the loss of a life partner. The author's honesty and ability to reflect on her experience is genuine and her compassion and empathy for the reader is very evident throughout the book.

She offers steps on what to do after a loss that are concrete, practical, and broken down into realistic usable steps, especially for a person who is overwhelmed and in shock. I could see reviewing those steps frequently and using them as a way to ground myself with a plan of action in the face of such a huge loss. Her ability to weave brain science and meditation in with her personal story is impressive.

— LORI EINHORN, EARLY CHILDHOOD EDUCATOR

Therese Marchitelli's book, *What Not To Do When Your Husband Dies*, is a delight to read. This book is a deep dive into grief and how our mind navigates it. Educational and practical, you will find nuggets of support in her exploration and her life experiences.

We will all face the beast of grief some time in our lives. Therese's vulnerable delve into her own journey is honest and raw. We can all learn from her mis-steps and her years of mindfulness and meditation. She beautifully takes us through the way our own brain works while 'on grief.' This practical guide is a missive for anyone experiencing grief, and honestly, for every one of us.

— JESSICA GOLDMUNTZ STOKES, AUTHOR OF
SEEKING CLARITY IN THE LABYRINTH: A
DAUGTHER'S JOURNEY THROUGH ALZHEIMER'S

T.J. Marchitelli's book is a wonderful blend of unadulterated memoir, (just enough) science and a "how to" guide for surviving and thriving through the deep soul-shattering loss of a loved one.

The beauty of this book is that it can also support ANY KIND of BIG LIFE CHANGE: the kind that shake us to our core, asking us to redefine who we are in the world and what the hell do we do now?

This book is especially relevant now, in a Post-Covid 19 World. How many of us have consciously grieved the losses of this collective wounding? Many of the book's strategies for healing "the brain on grief" are relevant to us ALL.

I truly appreciate Marchitelli's easy command of the science of the "brain on grief; " it also holds true for the "brain on trauma." It has given me context, insight and compassion for myself on own my life's journey. May it grant you the same freedom.

— FRANCES TREJO-LAY, AUTHOR OF *SANCTUARY* & *PLANTING THE SEED*

WHAT NOT TO DO WHEN YOUR HUSBAND DIES

WHAT NOT TO DO WHEN YOUR HUSBAND DIES

NEUROSCIENCE AND MINDFULNESS AS TOOLS TO NAVIGATE GRIEF

T.J. MARCHITELLI

Red Thread Publishing LLC. 2023

Write to **info@redthreadbooks.com** if you are interested in publishing with Red Thread Publishing. Learn more about publications or foreign rights acquisitions of our catalog of books: www.redthreadbooks.com

Paperback ISBN: I978-1-955683-86-9

Ebook ISBN: 978-1-955683-87-6

Cover Design: Red Thread Designs

Author Photo: Kris Giacobbe Photography

DEDICATION

*To my children, Ben and Gabrielle, whom I love dearly. To the light of joy
that they brought into our lives: David, their dad, Joe and Jenna and Dolly
and Tony, their grandparents and to mine. To the sadness I share with
them. I am eternally grateful for all they taught me with their brilliance,
wisdom, and love, even when it was hard to hear.*

*To David, my dear person, gone from this realm so many years ago. Too
young, too soon. I forever miss your smile, your humor, your gentleness
and quirkiness. Your legacy lives on through us; we miss you.*

*To my teacher, my guru, the Venerable Chögyam Trungpa, Rinpoche, a
dragon who brought the wisdom of Tibetan Buddhism to young Americans
searching for meaning. He showed me how to work with my mind, to tame
its wildness and train it to hold compassion, elegance, and dignity.*

*And to Shonté Jovan Taylor, the neuroscientist, my teacher and mentor,
without whose passion to bring an understanding of our magnificent brain
to humankind this book would still be a dream.*

My life has been shaped by all of you, and I am profoundly grateful.

XO

T.J. Marchitelli

CONTENTS

PART THREE
FINDING RESILIENCE

FOREWORD
SHONTÉ JOVAN TAYLOR

"Amidst the synapses and neurons, the brain holds the scars of our grief, but also the balm of our recovered joys and the roadmap to healing."
— Shonté Jovan Taylor, Neuroscientist

I am privileged to introduce you to an enlightening exploration of grief, healing, and the deeper understanding of our own minds. Grief is a universal emotion, yet the journey through it is profoundly personal. The pain we feel often leaves us seeking answers, desperate for solace and a path to healing. This is where the brilliance of Therese shines.

In the expanse of this book, not only will you delve into the neuroscience of grief and healing, but you will also confront the common mistakes many inadvertently make as they grapple with loss. Recognizing these pitfalls is the first step; forgiving oneself for stumbling into them is a vital part of the journey. Therese acknowledges that grief doesn't come with a manual, and mistakes are a part of our human process. She gently guides readers towards a place of self-forgiveness, emphasizing that it's not about perfection, but progress.

What sets this book apart is its revolutionary approach to understanding and navigating grief. Rather than offering platitudes or generalized advice, Therese provides insights into the 'why' of our emotions. By understanding the intricacies of our brain, we can better grasp why we feel the way we do and find more effective strategies for healing.

Grief is not a momentary challenge to overcome but a lifelong journey to embrace. Therese imparts the wisdom that to truly heal, one must curate a mindset that encompasses this journey. Throughout the chapters, she shares how to harness this mindset by understanding and using our brains more intentionally. Through healing tools and tangible plans, readers are guided to nurture themselves in every facet of their lives – mentally, spiritually, financially, socially, and physically. This holistic approach is a testament to her deep understanding of the multidimensional nature of healing.

The stories shared here not only serve as testimonials of the healing power of understanding and confronting our grief but also as a testament to our innate ability to rebuild and find joy again. Through each chapter, Therese gracefully bridges the gap between the mind's intricate processes and the heart's deep yearnings.

As a neuroscientist, I have witnessed the transformative power of understanding our minds at their core. I commend you, the reader, for embarking on this enlightening journey. Embrace the discomfort, welcome the revelations, and allow yourself to be transformed by the profound wisdom encapsulated in this book.

Thank you, Therese, for your pioneering spirit, courage, and commitment to lighting the path for those seeking understanding and healing. Your contribution to this realm of knowledge is not just a beacon of hope, but a testament to the resilience of the human spirit.

Embrace the journey, and let the profound process of healing and self-discovery begin.

PREFACE

As it unfolds, life is full of surprises. We can't really predict where its journey will take us. We become entrenched in our routines, in finding ourselves, in creating our goals and expressing our dreams. We take on different roles and throw ourselves into them: wife, husband, lover, partner, daughter, son, mother, father, friend, CEO, mentor. We really don't pay any attention to the transitoriness and the impermanence of our daily existence unless a sudden, probably tragic, change interrupts it. These life-changing losses span many things—it could be the death of our person, someone we loved or had a complicated relationship with but whose death dealt a blow to our life path. It could be a divorce, financial demise, job insecurity, selling a family home, being torn from your home country, retirement, leaving an abusive relationship, the state of our planet Earth, and so much more.

For me, it was the sudden tragic death of my husband, David. While David's death is the basis of this book, the story isn't just about him dying from the head injury he sustained in a car crash; it's also about the complicated process of dealing with life after his death. It's written with 20/20 hindsight vision, the vision and wisdom gained by deep reflection, age, and experience. When we are faced with the overwhelming experience of grief, we often stumble in the dark trying to find our way. For those of us who have lost a spouse, the world can feel like it has been turned upside down, the rudder on our ship has been destroyed by orcas or floating debris, and we're drifting in unknown waters. I made many mistakes during the first months and years after David's death despite having had a meditation practice for over 20 years and thinking that being able to calm my mind through mindfulness meditation was enough to get me through grief's hold.

This book is about how grief affects our brain and hijacks our mind. It asks what triggers our brain to go off track and how we can regain our balance and equilibrium, our direction, albeit something different than we might have envisioned had this loss trauma not derailed us. While grief is a universal experience that transcends time, culture, and circumstance, and an inevitable part of life, it remains one of the most challenging and isolating experiences we face. This book is an account of my missteps, the lessons I learned, and how the intersection of neuroscience and the knowledge of working with my mind through mindfulness meditation ultimately provided me with the understanding I was seeking in order to help others navigate their grief with clarity and resilience.

Who am I to be writing about this subject? My education as a social scientist has shaped my approach, driving me to incorporate evidence-based mindfulness practices and insights from neuroscience into this work. As an entrepreneur, I understand the importance of innovation and accessibility, ensuring that these techniques and ideas are presented in a relatable and digestible manner. As a widow, mother, end-of-life doula and neuro-grief and loss coach and trainer, I have come to understand the many forms and dimensions of grief.

What Not To Do When Your Husband Dies: Neuroscience and Mindfulness as Tools to Navigate Grief is a story about my journey, but it is also a guide for those who find themselves walking a similar path. It illustrates how the choices we make in the wake of loss can sometimes exacerbate our pain and perpetuate further grief.

It's not a book that came easy. I'm not the widow who started a non-profit around her loss, who declared herself and planted a banner, forging forward with a mission that would help her make sense of her loss, give purpose to her life. My grief journey was and still is a deep dive into the underpinnings of understanding grief as an entity. An entity that wants to talk. Wants to be heard and wants to be acknowledged. Grief is my companion. Sometimes smothering me with its demanding nature. Sometimes lying dormant, waiting, roiling beneath my consciousness. I became intrigued with her persistence to show up when least expected and send me on another wild ride. I invited her in and began to understand her and my unique journey with her. I've learned about grief through inquisitiveness, perseverance and the determination to be still with her complicated nature and let it unfold within me. Grief is a science. Her nature lies in the depths of our individual psyches.

In this book, you will find a blend of personal stories, research-based insights, and practical advice as I strive to help you, my dear reader, understand the ins and outs of your unique journey with grief and loss by sharing the poignancy of my grief journey and by highlighting the mistakes I made during the first several years. You will learn about the common pitfalls of grief and how to recognize them. Most importantly, you will gain a plan for taking care of yourself by surrounding yourself with the support you need. I hope to provide you with valuable tools to better understand your own journey and find a way to move forward with strength and grace. The hardest part is stepping into, embodying, and becoming friends with your grief.

You are not alone on this journey. There are many people who have walked this path, many resources and communities that have grown to support you as you embark on your own path of growth. It is my deepest hope that this book will serve as a beacon of light to guide you through the dark times and confusing emotions of grief and help you find a way to move forward and rebuild your life.

In memory of my beloved husband, and with gratitude for the lessons his death has taught me.

XO

T.J. Marchitelli

PROLOGUE

1977

It was 1977. I had returned to the east coast for my brother's wedding and to figure out if I should stay on the East Coast or go back to Boulder, where I had been living for several years. Living in Colorado, I missed water—the ocean, the rivers, and lakes of my native New Jerseyan upbringing. There were times during mountain hikes when I could smell the ocean. How weird was that? And there was The City. The City where I dreamed of living as a child whose bedroom window looked out over lower Manhattan. As a child, I had decided that 27 would be an exceptional year for me. Now here it was 1977 and my 27th year.

As I sat, surrounded by family and friends, at my brother's wedding, I realized my time in Boulder had come to an end. The East Coast was my heart, and New York City, with all it had to offer, was mine to uncover. It felt magical—moving to Manhattan, an island surrounded by water, and being 27! I was figuring it out; I had graduated from a university in 1972 with a B.A. in Social Science. Rather than pursue a career in social work, I decided to enroll in a two-year art school program, which led to my desire to engage with my whole body as an artistic form and hence my intrigue with the study of movement, specifically martial arts, and dance...which is what led me to Boulder and a contemplative dance program at a rather innovative new school called Naropa Institute (now Naropa University). It was at Naropa that I began my study of Tibetan Buddhism and meditation practice. A worldwide community was forming around the study of these teachings, and there was a center in Manhattan. I felt connected and at home.

Those of us who were drawn to the study and practice of Tibetan Buddhism were linked with the desire to learn about our minds, to center ourselves with meditation, and invoke wakefulness and higher levels of being. We were a community of practitioners and students who were also living and working and attending universities in New York City. We were young, "alive, awake, and digging everything."[1] This is where David and I met—this magical, open space. It was here we fell in love and here where his memorial service would be held. But I'm getting ahead of myself.

MANHATTAN

David was a staid member of the New York Buddhist community, I was a newcomer, and there were many people to meet and many friendships to form. I had first dates with different men in the community, but my first date with David was memorable. He took me to a Cuban-Chinese restaurant, a first for me! I don't remember its name, but the location was 14th Street between 6th and 7th Avenues. The food was sensational, the conversation deep, and our bond cemented. We became a "couple," one of many forming in our community. In the early spring of 1978, we moved into an apartment together on Riverside Drive. I had a job at an interior design firm on the upper east side, and David worked for a non-profit on the upper west side. Our nights and weekends were filled with different adventures in the city, dining at MiChinita, another Cuban-Chinese restaurant located in Chelsea, all curated by my personal concierge and tour guide, as David was a native New Yorker.

He had grown up in Manhattan, the only child of a Brooklyn College graduate chemistry professor and a history major who had worked on the Manhattan Project. David knew all the best places to eat, and our weekends were filled with excursions to the many different neighborhoods of NYC. Life was grand, but finances kept us from enjoying everything we wanted to explore. Interior design became stale. I wanted a better opportunity to advance in my career. My thought was, *"Where do I go to make money?"* The answer came to me in a flash, Wall Street. I found a position in the research department of a small investment banking company and eventually became a research associate and stockbroker.

Meanwhile, David had decided to get a master's degree, an MBA in finance. Ironic, I thought, since his undergraduate degree was in fiction writing. We laughed about that. David was a nerd and a genius. He had a perfect score on his math SATs and near-perfect on the English portion. David was accepted to Harvard Business School but chose the newly established business school at NYU. I was perplexed by his decision but understood his reluctance to leave NYC for Boston.

After attaining his MBA, David was hired by NYLife Insurance Company and served as their fledgling Venture Capital Department analyst. It was here that David presented NYLife with the investment opportunity that made history—literally!! On David's recommendation, NYLIfe invested $1 million in The Discovery Channel. He then convinced them to invest another $12 million to see the project and vision through. NYLife made 24 times their money with that investment, and David became the sought-after person to help get a project on 'cable TV. Remember, this was the early 1980s. The availability of a public internet was a good decade away.

David and I were married in 1979. In early 1982, we talked about starting a family and decided to wait a year. Our son was born about ten months later. We had that conversation again in late 1984 and once again decided to wait a year. Our daughter was born about ten months later. We agreed never to have that conversation again, although we were open to more children. I debated about continuing my Wall Street career but, in the end, decided to take time off to be with our babies. It was a mutual decision, one that was open-ended.

As you can tell by this story, ours was a life headed for happily-ever-after. Young family, David's rising career, love, and fun. As our children got older, we started to look at moving to the suburbs. It would mean David commuting to the city and me staying in the suburbs taking care of our two kids. In the end, we bought a vacation and weekend home in East Hampton and eventually moved our family there. This is where the unraveling begins.

David eventually left NYLife and started a venture capital firm. We set up an office in the basement of our home, and since I had a financial background, I became his first assistant. As his business grew, he was able to hire someone more suitable for the job. Life was good. East Hampton was an easy community to fit into. The schools were excellent and our children were happy. As David's business grew, his work began to take him away on trips throughout the country and internationally. The children and I became accustomed to his travel and looked forward to the weeks and weekends when he could join us at the beaches and festivities that were typical of life in the Hamptons. With both kids in school and a husband that traveled, I wanted to go back to work. I decided that getting my real-estate license would give me the flexibility I needed to satisfy my career needs and to keep our domestic life running smoothly.

Here we were, living in the Hamptons, a privileged place to be.

EAST HAMPTON, SEPTEMBER 4, 1995

Another Labor Day weekend in the Hamptons was upon us, and it was **upon** us. In the late '80s, East Hampton was still the "poor relation" compared to the rest of the towns that comprised the Hamptons, which not only meant the "summer people" left and it was less crowded in the fall and winter, but also that life slowed down, and we were able to enjoy the tranquility of the area. In 1987, East Hampton's Main Street boasted many "mom and pop" stores and a fledgling "Barefoot Contessa" on Newtown Lane. Though the population increased in the summer, there was still ample parking at the town beaches.

It was now 1995, and, wow, the feeling had changed. The population in the Hamptons had grown exponentially. East Hampton had become another neighborhood of Manhattan: lines, traffic, higher prices, and the aggressive nature of the speediness of it all.

So here we were, Labor Day weekend, 1995. Since David traveled a lot for business, we liked an "open" plan on weekends. Our son was twelve, and our daughter was nine and approaching her tenth birthday. We were all happy to hang out together, go to the beach, and have a family weekend. School was beginning right after Labor Day, and both excitement and regret were in the air.

Our family often spent several weeks over the summer in the Northeast Kingdom of Vermont attending programs at a renowned meditation center that was part of our spiritual community. That summer of 1995, we rented a house for the month of July, and while David thought he would be there most of the month, his work demanded otherwise. The kids and I spent the month in a house that was "off-the-grid," mostly without David being there. It felt like a star-crossed situation, but I tried to make the best of it. It was during that month on a weekend when David was there, driving down a dirt road and admiring the beauty of the countryside, when he asked, "Do you want to put an extension on our house in East Hampton or move to Vermont?" Was that a trick question, I thought, and I immediately responded with "Move to Vermont." Our children agreed. A family decision was made on the spot. We had been tossing this idea around for some time given the rapidly increasing level of materialism and the materialistic outlook in the Hamptons and the desire to get our kids away from that. With the help of recent technology, David felt he could work from virtually anywhere. Vermont also offered an excellent high school for our kids. We contacted a real estate agent and began looking at properties. At the end of the month, we returned to East Hampton, excited by our decision to move. David returned to Vermont for two weeks in August to attend a meditation program and revisit some of the properties we had looked at together.

Back to Labor Day weekend. I don't remember what we did every day of that weekend, but it included lounging around the swimming pool, going to the ocean, and hanging out with friends. Typical summer beach-house stuff. I do remember Labor Day itself. We decided to make a day of it at the beach, but we got a late start, and by the time we got to our favorite beach, we couldn't find parking. We drove to a residents-only beach and managed to find a spot. The beach was more packed than I had ever experienced. It offered no reprieve from the crowded conditions in the Hamptons. There wasn't an off-season anymore; everyone knew about the "secret" shortcuts to avoid Route 27 (the two-lane highway that led through the Hamptons and out to Montauk (aka The End); the lack of parking for shopping; the lines in the supermarkets; the mom and pop stores being replaced by designer stores and the prices! We smiled smugly at our decision to move to Vermont. Yay for us!

We spent several hours at the beach that day, enjoying the ocean air; our daughter and David—true beach lovers—took a long walk together while our son and I relaxed on beach chairs and read. I took photos of the kids, but David was off swimming and by the time he came back to our blanket, I had put the camera away. We left in the late afternoon, happy and content.

David and I had dinner plans with another couple that night, and our kids would be cared for by a family friend. It was a fitting end to a rather chaotic summer.

MILK FOR THE MORNING

We arrived home from our dinner date shortly after 9:00 p.m. Our kids were content and watching a movie. As I got ready for initiating their bedtimes, I went into the kitchen, opened the refrigerator and noticed we were out of milk. "I forgot to get milk today. We have no milk for the morning." I announced out loud. "I'll go get it," David replied.

I went upstairs to change my clothes. I was just about to tell David not to go out for milk and that I would get it in the morning when I heard the kitchen door open and his voice saying, "I'm going to get milk." "You don't have to," I thought but I failed to voice the words in time. I heard the door close behind him. I finished changing and went to get our daughter ready for bed. It was about 9:30 pm.

With my daughter settled, I joined my son to watch the end of the movie. Time passed. I looked at the clock; it was getting late....maybe 10:30. I wondered what was keeping David. A little while later, I heard a car pull into the driveway, it was white—the same color as David's—and I was relieved that he was home. I waited for him to come in, but the kitchen door didn't open. Odd, I thought, the car was idling in our driveway, but David hadn't come into the house. I went outside to see what was happening. As I stepped onto the porch, I saw that although the car was white, it wasn't David's. To make matters worse, when the car door opened, a policeman stepped out. "Oh no!" I thought, "David's been arrested because he wouldn't take a breathalyzer test." (There had been an increase in the local police randomly stopping cars and giving breathalyzer tests to drivers, and I knew David would not stand for such an action.) I sighed, somewhat in relief.

"Mrs. Glickstein?" the officer asked. "Yes," I replied. "There's been an accident." I could feel the ground drop from below me. From that moment on, the night took on a surreal quality as uncertainty and shock engulfed me. The officer was communicating with someone else via his radio. "Do you have children?" he asked. "Yes." "Can you get someone to come and stay with them?" "OK." He told me that David had been in an accident on Swamp Road, that he was being taken to Southampton Hospital, and could I get there soon. Wait. No, David was being airlifted to Stony Brook Hospital, about an hour from where we lived, I needed to go there. Airlifted. Airlifted. Those words rang in my head. Airlift. An ominous word.

WITHOUT WARNING

Shock is interesting. It's like being once removed from what's right in front of you. In a way, it's protective; it's a neurochemical reaction by our body's regulatory system to keep us safe in treacherous, threatening circumstances, releasing hormones and chemicals that can trigger the fight, flight, freeze, or fawn response. The shock of hearing a police officer saying, "there's been an accident." The shock of having the ground fall out from beneath you. The shock of moving between wanting to fall apart and knowing that you need to be organized. Find someone to stay with our kids, and drive an hour to a hospital further away from me because he was being (oh goodness) airlifted from the local hospital to another one. Stay steady, breathe. Panic was the last thing I needed to take over right now; that would come later.

I called several friends and left messages, and finally reached one who was home. I explained what had happened and that I needed someone to stay with our children so I could drive to Stony Brook Hospital. It was nearly 11:00 p.m when all of the friends I had called converged on our house. It was decided that some would stay with our kids, and the others would drive me to the hospital. I called David's parents. We left for Stony Brook shortly after 11:00 p.m.

We arrived at the hospital around midnight. It was at that same time that the helicopter arrived with David. It was concerning that the airlift had taken so long to arrive from Southampton to Stony Brook. When we checked into the emergency room, we were asked to stay in the waiting area while they assessed and processed David. It seemed like an inordinate amount of time. We kept checking with the nurse, and finally, around 2:00 a.m. we were allowed to see David. His head and eyes were swollen beyond imagination. The nurse on duty said she saw a change in the monitors when David heard our voices and that she thought he knew we were there. She told us David needed surgery, and a surgeon was on the way to assess his injury. Shortly thereafter, the surgeon arrived and examined David. David needed brain surgery. The surgeon told us that the surgery would probably last for five hours. When I looked at the clock, it was 3:00 a.m. The surgery would last until at least 8:00 a.m. We were shown to a waiting area with a telephone that I could use to call family and friends. I began the process of calling people who were near and dear to David and me. In the meantime, we waited. We offered support to one another that David was young, strong, and he would pull through. "He will be okay," our friend said with tears in his eyes. To this day, I remember those words and the feeling that came over me. Our friend was so positive that David would pull through, and I felt so sad for all of us if David didn't.

Around 5:00 a.m., the waiting room door opened, and to our surprise, the surgeon came in. "I've done all I can," he said. It was not comforting to hear those words or realize, in fact, that the 5-hour surgery had been completed in 2 hours. I had a sinking feeling throughout my body as the room slowly dissolved around me.

David was brain-dead. He died from the traumatic brain injury he received when his head met the roof of the car that had caved in when his car wrapped around the tree that he hit. He was taken off life support and took his last breath at 3:20 p.m. on Tuesday, September 5, 1995. He had been surrounded by friends and family, all of whom were in a waiting room a few doors from where he lay. It was only me, the surgeon, and a nurse in the room when he took his last breath. He was 42 years old. It was the saddest day of my life. A numbness crept over me as I looked at David's body. A corpse. I was reminded of lines from a Buddhist text that reads, "Death comes without warning, this body will be a corpse." I wasn't ready for this. For dear, sweet David to be a corpse. I was a widow. Life had changed in a breath. The sudden shock to all of us who knew and loved him. The sudden life change for my children and me.

UNDERSTANDING OUR BRAIN ON GRIEF

"No one ever told me that grief feels so much like fear."

— *CS LEWIS*

Breathe, I told myself, just breathe. I was really good at that—the meditation instruction to breathe, be, let go of thoughts, allow space. What I wasn't good at was engaging with the "dust" before it settled, or getting sucked into reaction. What was missing? Why did I keep going around in this same mind loop? Using mindfulness meditation techniques to quell my emotional brain, to unseat the reactiveness for the moment. It became a familiar labyrinth, a habitual pattern that I could see, I could identify, but I couldn't find the center of. Feeling close to being grounded, centered in the labyrinth, only to find myself on the outer edges, riding the emotional roller coaster that is the mind of a grieving person. Through my desire to understand what was hijacking my mind, I began to hear and read about doctors using brain scans to look at the brains of meditators and about neuroscientists making significant advancements in understanding the brain and its systems. There were answers there, I could feel it.

Before we get into the nitty gritty of the mistakes I made while in the throes of grief, I want to provide some information about our brain to illustrate (1) how grief affects the brain's systems and (2) how that impacts our ability to have clarity of mind. This was an eye opener for me. Understanding how our brain processes grief gave me insight into where and why I became "stuck" in my grief and made decisions that further derailed my life and the lives of my children. My wish is that this information will benefit your life.

We can attract people and things into our lives if our intentions are strong; we can magnetize people who are essential to our understanding and growth. It was my great fortune to be introduced to and study with the neuroscientist Shonté Jovan Taylor, who has devoted her time and expertise to helping people understand how the brain works so that they can use it in their work to inspire and help others. My knowledge and understanding of the brain and how grief affects it would not be possible without her mentoring.

We know that grief can have a hold on us emotionally, physically, intellectually, and spiritually. It changes us socially. It has an energy of its own and can cause us to feel hijacked by its power, our lives held hostage and derailed. All of these seemingly random responses that touch every aspect of our lives can be traced back to how grief affects our brain. Grief brain hijacks our mind. It makes us feel detached, lacking focus and clarity. It creates brain fog, memory loss, uncertainty, and the inability to make decisions.

To understand what grief does to you psychosomatically, we are going to look at how our brain works, how it functions, and how all of that relates to our body and our mind. How do you make decisions when in a state of grieving? How do you make choices that will prove to be a beneficial direction for your life? How do you involve yourself in your life, be present in it and for it? It's hard not to let sadness and grief and the ordinary tasks of everyday living overwhelm you. There are so many questions that we must decide to look at and not let the fear of the answer prevent us from answering. We can look at the state of our mind, and our emotional brain from the position of being the CEO of our life. This puts our whole brain into action and directs the brain's energy into our higher-level thinking. We get there with compassion for our grief; compassion for our emotional, limbic system; and compassion for the fight, flight, freeze, or fawn system *(see Appendix 1)* that can be triggered. That system is a function of the brain that wants to keep us safe, to protect us. That system has been set into action from the chaos being thrust upon us by the release of stress hormones into our system. We can take a simple understanding of how our brain is processing the shock of the death of our person and use that to make sense of why grief has taken hold of our life. This is not meant as a training in neuroscience; it's meant to provide a simple understanding of which parts of the brain are most affected by grief. This is by no means the whole picture of the brain and its integrated systems.

FOLLOWING IS A LIST OF WHAT WE'LL COVER:

- **The brain stem** – instinctive, survival mode, unconscious regulation
- **The limbic system** – emotional brain comprised of: — **The amygdala** — traditionally called the fear center, stimulated by novelty —**The hippocampus** – memory center
- **The anterior cingulate cortex** – emotional regulation center
- **The prefrontal cortex** – higher-level thinking center, CEO — **The right hemisphere** – creative center — **The left hemisphere** – analytical center

"Cells that fire together, wire together."
— *Hebb's Axiom*[1]

Our brain is made up of billions of cells and ninety million miles of pathways. Quite impressive! It also has different regions that take on specific functions of our existence. For as long as humans have been surviving on planet Earth, our brain has been evolving from very primitive primal responses and functions to the more complex regions of what we can call higher brain functioning. The parts of the brain that we'll primarily focus on are the brain stem, the limbic system, and the prefrontal cortex. These areas involve instinct, love, hate, memory, and higher-level thinking.

THE INSTINCTIVE OR LIZARD BRAIN: THE BRAIN STEM

The base of our brain, the brain stem, is connected to our spine through various nerve systems. The brain stem is the most ancient and primitive part of the brain and regulates all of our automatic bodily functions, such as heart rate, blood pressure, and breathing. It oversees the flow of our energy from our brain to our body and from our body to our brain. It responds to threats against our safety, stimulates the release of stress and other hormones, and can throw us into fight, flight, freeze, or fawn reactions. The brain perceives the death of our person as a significant endangerment. Our life has been altered, leaving us vulnerable. Grief can leave us scared and reactive, all too willing to jump into a habitual response. Run, stay put, protect, give in. By understanding the intensity of energy and feeling flowing from the brain stem as it reacts to a situation, we can become aware of its influence on a conscious level. How to do this? Give yourself a five-second pause, regroup before making a decision or speaking, reevaluate—is this a realistic response? If there's a dragon at your doorstep, it might very well be; otherwise, breathe. Breathe and take a minute to assess your situation, get out of your head and into your heart center, allow space, call on one of your board members (see page 29 for more details). You don't have to shoulder anything on your own if you set up a Board of Trust-eds. Our brain is a "pattern-finding" machine. Consciously finding the pattern of our habitual wiring can help us process emotions and regulate instinctive responses to the uncertainty of our changed life. We can learn to shift our mental energy and take bold steps while grieving our loss.

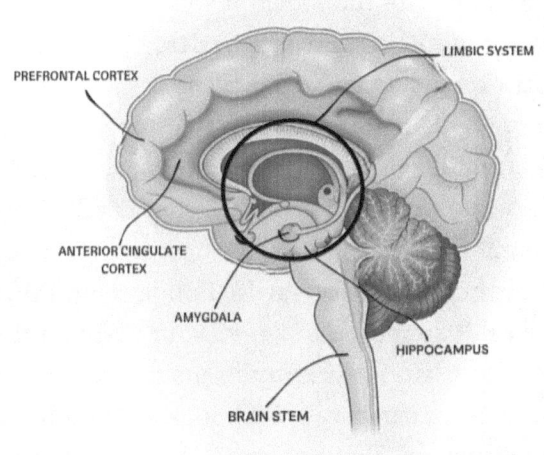

THE EMOTIONAL BRAIN: THE LIMBIC SYSTEM

Our limbic system is often referred to as the emotional center of our brain and is interconnected to many of the brain's regions. For our purpose, we'll focus on the amygdala—including its interconnectedness to the brain stem—and the hippocampus.

The amygdala rules our emotions, emotional behavior and motivation. It also stores emotional associations that relate to specific memories. Trauma, fear, anxiety, stress and, believe it or not, too much relaxation activate the amygdala and allow instinctive responses to prevail. It processes and is often activated by the brain stem's energy. Is there a threat? Am I safe to sleep soundly? This can be good if there is a physical threat and you need to get out of the way of danger. It can be debilitating if the threat is grief-induced anxiety about how you're going to move forward with your life without your person.

The hippocampus plays a role in learning, and in processing and consolidating short-term memory into long-term memory. It serves as the short-term memory center of the emotional brain. The amygdala can generate memories that involve fear, stress, and negativity into the hippocampus. The hippocampus can likewise activate an amygdala response with certain memories. For instance, we're suddenly grief-stricken when we're at a place we've been to with our person. A memory about a time we were there together is triggered *(see Appendix 2)*, and, in this place where we once existed together, we face the stone-cold reality that our person has died and we are here without them. I think this is why we have such grief bursts and triggers around birthdays, anniversaries, holidays, and future milestones. Our life wasn't supposed to be without them on those occasions. Our emotional brain is also more sensitive to fear and threat than it is to reward. If we can take a fresh look at our grief, breathing through it, being curious about what it brings up, sitting with gentleness and compassion toward ourselves, we can keep our minds from being hijacked. Understanding this information won't put an end to our grief, but it might give us the breathing space to ride its wave without succumbing to its force. We can be conscious of thoughts that activate our hippocampus and amygdala. Oftentimes, when our amygdala is activated, our prefrontal cortex is less active. However, new research has found that the amygdala is also stimulated by novelty and curiosity. This is a more holistic view that goes beyond the traditional "fight or flight" paradigm that it's often associated with. Its role is really multifaceted. In other words, the amygdala can stimulate and be stimulated by both the fear center and the higher executive functioning of our brain. The different regions of our brain interact and communicate with each other in a dynamic and interconnected manner to regulate emotional and physiological responses.

THE ANTERIOR CINGULATE CORTEX (ACC): EMOTIONAL REGULATION

The ACC helps us process uncomfortable emotions. It connects with both the prefrontal cortex and the limbic system and plays an important role in regulating an emotional hijack by the amygdala. We've gone "limbic" when the limbic system has taken over and our emotions are riding us, when we're emotionally reactive to experiences and situations that we might ordinarily not react to so strongly. Uncontrollable sobbing, staying in bed all day, not wanting to leave the house, are all normal reactions of grief, attached to feelings generated by loss. When our energies are being subverted by the more primitive parts of our brain, our ability to function is impaired.

THE PREFRONTAL CORTEX: HIGHER-LEVEL EXECUTIVE FUNCTIONING

The prefrontal cortex (PFC) is the CEO of our brain. When we're planning things, setting goals, and making well-informed, whole-brain-based decisions, our PFC is switched on. This area of our brain is located behind our eyes. It's our wisdom center and uses much of our brain's mental energy. When we're grieving, most of our mental energy is used up by our limbic system in trying to figure out and process the death of our person. Our brain has made innumerable neural connections around someone who is no longer alive. It's distressing, regardless of the relationship we had with them, and our brain is subconsciously searching for that person, using up energy.

One of the major complaints about grief is brain fog. Brain fog is feeling dazed and confused, not remembering things. While you don't have to be grieving to feel these, to me there's a correlation between the energy siphon from the PFC by the limbic system. How can we see all our options, know what our choices are, and make good decisions if we don't have enough energy to fuel our PFC? How do we pull this all together, tame our emotional mind, and make new neuronal pathways that spark our resilience? Let's take a look at the two hemispheres that make up our brain. Each of these control different functions. For instance, our left brain is said to be our language center, for verbal communication, and our right brain is our visual center, for nonverbal communication.

RIGHT BRAIN/LEFT BRAIN

We've all heard the theories about being right-brain or left-brain dominant. Truth is, we use both our right and left brain because our brain is wired that way. There are many pathways that intertwine between the two. We probably all have an understanding that our right hemisphere is involved with more artistic, visionary, creative, and intuitive thinking. When we see diagrams of the brain divided into right and left hemispheres, it's the right hemisphere that's painted with bright colors. We could say that the right brain puts the color in our lives. ·

Our left hemisphere is our analytical side. It's our more logical and rational side. Strategic planning, detail-oriented. We often associate left-brain thinking with math and science.

So how does this all relate to our journey with grief?

Neuronal pathways grow because the brain likes shortcuts, which can be understood as direct pathways to the task at hand. The brain's shortcuts help us process and organize information efficiently. They allow us to quickly solve problems and assess situations. Efficiency conserves the brain's energy, but there's another side to this: the brain is also pretty lazy, and this "laziness" can produce shortcuts or patterns of behavior that don't serve us.

In grief, our brain's energy is being used up by our emotional and instinctual brain regions. Very little is going to rational decision-making, strategic planning, and connecting with our intuition. To make matters worse, our mental shortcuts, even on a good day, can often lead us to make rash decisions because the nature of a shortcut circumvents other pathways. For the brain, these other pathways are the ones that might lead us to use our PFC and make better, whole-brain-based decisions. So here we go: Brain fog, check. Forgetfulness, check. Not being able to concentrate, check. Fear of not making good decisions, check. Physical, emotional, intellectual, spiritual distress, check. It's not only that bad decisions are made from being emotionally reactive, they can also be made through the habitual "laziness" that can be attributed to the shortcuts in our brain's circuitry.

We can grieve many different things (*see Appendix 3.)*, not only the death of someone we love. Any kind of life change can cause us to grieve. Our life has changed and we're learning how to navigate the changes. And when these changes are happening, our brain is making adjustments to our neuronal pathways.

In the next section we'll explore the antidotes to our brain's obstacle course by looking at the mistakes I made early on in my grief over David's death and applying the understanding how and why grief traps the brain.

66

How to calm a fearful brain: The PFC (aka CEO, boss brain) is the most modern part of our brain and uses up the most energy...in a good way. The more energy we give our PFC, the less energy goes to the more primitive parts of the brain. Planning, organizing and goal setting are all functions that the PFC loves. These activities help to deactivate the amygdala because they create a sense of certainty, and the amygdala sees certainty as being safe. Setting a few simple tasks or goals for your day gives the amygdala a sense of safety as well as optimizes the health of our PFC. Working on a project or towards a goal on a daily basis, no matter how small it is—for instance writing in a journal for 10 minutes— redefines our brain by creating new neuronal pathways, which can become new habits and better ways of organizing our lives. This is known as neuroplasticity. It takes work and time, mindfulness and awareness of our habitual tendencies, and a plan to shift our brain's energy to our executive functioning.

99

PART ONE
GROUND

*"Helping someone else through difficulty
is where civilization starts."*
— *Margaret Mead*

I

THE AFTERMATH OF LOSS
STUMBLING IN THE DARK

I knew there were things to be done now. Things to get right or wrong. But this was free fall, free throw, free for all. Watching David take his last breath was an elevator dropping 100 stories with me on it. What now? What's to become of...life. My life, our children, his parents, my parents. What a nightmare to have landed at my door. Was I prepared for this moment? In some sense, yes, I was. After all, I had been studying and practicing Tibetan Buddhism with a Tibetan master for 20 years, contemplating impermanence, studying the mind, taming, and training it for uncertainty. Surely I would be able to compose myself during this unwanted and unchartered journey into widowhood. That was my attitude and mindset. I was strong, I was resilient, I was young and coming into my feminine power.

We lose a lot of things when our life partner dies. What I didn't realize was I had lost myself long before David died. That's what became clear. I had lost myself in the everydayness of domesticity. My life had become an autopilot event, a comfortable, safe life. Sure, it had its share of drama and concern, but on the whole, our little family had a happy, progressive existence. And that existence had just exploded. Widowhood is a different dimension, impossible to prepare for no matter how resilient and strong you are. Which is exactly how I made my first mistake. I had lost track of who I was or could be outside of my family bubble. Reeling from the impact of grief, I had to make decisions that I truly wasn't emotionally prepared for.

Breathe, I told myself, just breathe. Small steps, and if it doesn't feel right, stop. The days to come would demand things of me that I was unprepared for. Ordinary things, arrangements, decisions, our children's needs. David's death was a shock to all who knew him, especially our close meditation community. Friends in the community took charge of arranging things: a memorial service, the coffin, the cremation, and several Buddhist ceremonies. Offering condolences, bringing food, dinners. Inviting us to be with them without David. I am eternally grateful for the kindness of these friends and many others.

People will rise to an occasion. People will surround you and your family with love and kindness. It's what we do as humans. The essence of our humanity doesn't want to see anyone suffering. Here I was, here we were, my children and I, David's parents and I, in a place we didn't want to be. Pushed into something uncomfortable, not only uncomfortable for us but for our family and friends as well because, as everyone knew, after several weeks, no matter who they are, no matter how close they are, people need to return to their lives, and we are left to deal with our shattered world by ourselves. There is no blame in this. Still, I needed support from trusted friends and it was a mutual situation of confusion. I didn't know what kind of support I needed to ask for, and they didn't know how to reach out and offer their help. After all, we were all grieving David's sudden death in our own unique way.

2

MISTAKE #1:

GOING SOLO

There are a lot of tasks to deal with during the first several months of your bereavement, including funeral arrangements; financial and insurance paperwork; filing death certificates; closing bank accounts; opening bank accounts; and just plain juggling life, work, and children. It was no different for me. Where could I find support for myself and my children, our home environment, health, finances, and my real estate career? The support I had in those first few weeks was gone. My children had returned to school, and I was left to sort things out at home. What should I do with David's business, his clothing? How could I help his parents as they grieved the death of their only child? I knew that this first year was critical to just being and letting us settle into our new life, our life devoid of David.

In general, making decisions and weighing options is hard enough in good circumstances. For those who have lost their partner to death, they become rocky mountain cliffs to scale alone, leaving you vulnerable to more life-altering challenges and changes. I had to make several crucial decisions during that first year, which became some of the biggest mistakes I ever made in my life. Most of these mistakes stemmed from not having a support system in place that included the many different components of living and taking care of my life. My finances, my children, my nutrition, my physical and mental health care, my spirituality, and my social connections. Having people who continue to support you and engage with you through your grief journey doesn't happen automatically. It takes structure, strategy, and effort on your part to put it into place. I know this is hard. While you feel you don't have the bandwidth or the clarity to put this into action, it is necessary. It's the key to having the best possible outcome for you and your children, if any, as you transition into this change in your life path. What's needed in these first few months after your person's death is putting together a network of support for yourself. I call this creating a "Board of Trust-eds." It's meant to surround you with the kind of help and support you need in specific areas of your life. It's meant as guidance and a strategy to give you the best possible result as you move forward with your grief journey and your life. You can look at this as if you are the head of your own entrepreneurial enterprise: *Your Life Moving Forward, Inc.* You are the CEO of Your Life Moving Forward and your Board of Trust-eds are in place to help and support you with critical decision-making and finding balance in your life.

3

INTRODUCTION TO THE BOARD OF TRUST-EDS

Setting up a Board of Trust-eds ensures that you are not making major decisions about your life before you've seriously thought them through, explored your options, and talked about them with someone else. **Involvement** is the key here. A Board of Trust-eds is strategically inviting input into your life. It's solicited advice, a council, very different from someone giving you unsolicited feedback or advice on the fly. When I look back on it, there were several friends who tried to advise me "on the fly." I wish I had listened to some of it. I wish I had set it up differently so their advice didn't fall flat on the ground because I couldn't understand that I was in need of help. Believe me, you need help. **You need help and support** through the first year or two of your new life from a circle of people who care and from professionals who can advise you about critical decision-making. This will help you create a foundation for moving forward into the following years.

In general, you might consider the following types of people to be members of your board:

- **A financial advisor** – a professional and objective voice who you will seriously take advice from.
- **A spiritual advisor** – someone you can talk to who supports you spiritually, whatever your spiritual path may be.
- **A social worker or bereavement counselor.**
- **A widow doula** – someone who has walked in your shoes, who can offer the kind of guidance and support that comes with the experience of having gone through it.
- **A good friend** who will have lunch or dinner with you on a regular basis, or go for a walk.
- **A male or female counterbalance** for you and your children (council of dads or moms). In other words, if your child lost their father, do you have a male family member or friend who you trust to be a "father" figure for them? The same is true if they lost their mother. Do you have a female family member or friend you trust to be a "mother" figure for them? This is not something that needs to happen right away, but can be extra support for you if you're having trouble helping your child with their grief. This is not meant to replace their deceased parent.
- **A business person or coach** to talk to about your job or a business you want to launch.
- **A personal caregiver** such as a massage therapist, aesthetician, chiropractor, or yoga teacher.
- **A primary care physician.**
- **A handyman/woman** – someone you can call on in a pinch to help with small maintenance issues in your home.

When talking to those you trust and are going to invite to your board, you must ask for a one-year commitment. Write a contract,* something simple with your needs defined. Introduce the board members to each other, talk about the defined roles each of them is going to hold to empower them. You might want to meet with them, as a full group, once a week to begin with. Have an agenda, include what you're struggling with and let them add to it. They might have insights into how they feel they can support you and how they see their position, their role on your board. Set a time—how long will these meetings last (and it's ok if they go longer as long as everyone agrees). You can also meet with specific board members individually if the position they're fulfilling is front and foremost on your "my house is on fire" list. (*See Appendix 4 for sample contract.)

And really, dear, you will often feel that your house is on fire and you are a one-person bucket brigade. So get your board set up, pronto.

> Mistake #1 I was used to making decisions for myself. It had been part of my experience throughout my life, and these are the neuronal pathways that I had developed from childhood. I grew up relying on my ability to figure things out and move forward. This would be no different, or so I thought. Plus, my thinking went, I had my meditation practice to ground me. I could do this. What I hadn't anticipated was how grief turns your mind and your brain upside down, inside out, and is a roller-coaster ride of your emotional states of being. Thinking I would be able to navigate decisions, take care of my children's well being, support my grieving in-laws, and others who were affected by David's death without help was a grievous mistake. I was perfectly able to settle my mind through meditation, and I thought that was enough. It was not. We can become our own obstacles in any part of life, but this is especially true when grief has us in its stronghold. The remedy or antidote for this is creating a support system for yourself. A Board of Trust-eds.

4

CREATING AND ORGANIZING YOUR BOARD OF TRUST-EDS

"The best way to take care of the future
is to take care of the present moment."
— Thich Nhat Hanh

What I didn't understand or acknowledge back then but became clear over the years is that I had more options and choices than I thought I had. If I had put a Board of Trust-eds in place, I probably would have been able to pull my options out of my subconscious mind. Instead, I got into flight mode, and then freeze mode, and eventually, fawn response. Part of my undoing was my belief that I was independent, resilient, and financially okay. My strengths became my vulnerabilities.

Going it solo in widowhood is hard work, and it's debilitating. There's a lot to figure out and possibly some life-changing decisions to make. Before you set up your Board of Trust-eds, it's essential to understand and make a list of what your present needs are. What are the categories? Are there options for any of them? What's your strategy for each option? This type of reasoning will help you determine the best person for the position, as well as give you ideas or "talking points" about how to approach asking them so they understand how serious you are about enlisting their support.

After all, this isn't just about getting through the first year; it's about finding direction for the rest of your life. Make a plan, don't drift along. Be awake in this thing called grief and its subsequent mourning, that's engulfed your life and stolen your footing. Uncover your options; you have more "luminous doorways" than you think. This is an essential part of maneuvering the waters of the first year of widowhood.

Now that you've had some time to think about the different types of people for members of your Board, let's go into more detail about what those positions would involve. You can add others that are meaningful to you if you wish.

SELF CARE

Self care involves physical health as well as emotional and mental health. This position is best filled by two people:

1. Your primary care physician and, if needed, a grief coach, therapist, or counselor.
2. A person who cares about you and is willing to check in with you frequently via texts or phone calls, someone who has your back in the first few months after your loss. This can be a rotating position among board members.

SOCIAL RELATIONSHIPS

Maintaining your connection to the meaningful people in your life and your immediate world is necessary. This can be very hard and might be the last thing you have the energy for. At first, you will have many offers of support and help. People mean well but you will soon take a back burner to their lives. It really does require you to have a structure to keep your friends and family involved with your situation. Hence, this position can be seen as a "social director" who helps you create a structure, guides you, and reaches out to your people with you. It involves planning for fun, creative activities and adventures to keep you from feeling isolated and slipping into that "bottom of the barrel" feeling. If you have children, it can include playdates with their friends, adventures, and day trips that keep the joy in their lives and help to make new happy memories.

CHILDREN'S CARE

This role oversees a child's or teen's self-care. They need the same kind of organized involvement as you. Check in often with their primary care physician. Are there any peer support groups that you can bring them to? *(See Resources for children's grief groups.)* Children and teens need to feel connected to the world around them. Invite their input into adventures and activities that they might enjoy. Planning for their future is important. What are their needs going to be like in two years, three years, five years? Getting a sense of this as you plan with your board can alleviate a lot of stress as the years spin by.

FINANCES

Creating a strategic plan about your finances, regardless of the amount of money and other assets you have on hand, requires whole-brain, executive thinking. It will cut the amount of stress and emotional worry you might feel and help you to think creatively about the resources and options available to you. Even if you've been left with a comfortable amount of money to live on for the foreseeable future, you must fill this position with an objective trusted advisor who might not be the same person as your financial planner.

CAREER & PURPOSE

Are you an employee of a small business, academic institution, health organization, corporation, etc.? Do they understand workplace grief? Do you understand workplace grief? Is your employer open to understanding how grief affects the workplace? Do they have a grief policy in place? HR would be the department to ask about that. If you are self-employed with entrepreneurial tendencies, are you supported by others in your field? Or maybe you have a tight budget and losing your partner just made the situation worse. Do not be discouraged. There are safety nets in most communities for people who find themselves at their wit's end after the death of a key person in their life. Your area's social services can help direct you to the right resources.

This is an important area to take a deep look at with someone who can genuinely help you with uncovering options, discovering what each option has to offer, and creating a plan with directives and steps that will help you succeed.

SPIRITUAL PRACTICE

Whatever religion you choose to pursue, I recommend adding the practice of a mindfulness breath meditation to your spiritual ritual. The definition of meditation is to engage in mental exercise. Getting caught up in any kind of thought is actually meditation.You are meditating on whatever it is that's occupying your mind and, if you focus on it long enough, it can create neuronal pathways that can activate different areas of your brain. Using the breath as the object for meditation can take you out of your spinning and worrisome thoughts and ground you in the present moment and in the comfort of your body. You move out of your head and into your heart center. Focusing on your breath as a meditation practice helps you physically, emotionally, and mentally by calming and regulating stress hormones and brain regions. Check in with the leader of your church, temple, or meditation center; perhaps there is someone in that community who you can invite to your board. If you're unsure about how to include a mindfulness practice into your life, there are also many good online meditation teachers and groups that offer meditation instruction and classes.

It might feel overwhelming to create a board for your life especially now when you're trying to come to terms with living without your person but, if you do this, it will help you with your grief journey in many ways. Besides, you can look at "overwhelm" as either a lack of commitment or a lack of preparation. And "preparing" your life in this way actually helps your brain by moving energy to your prefrontal cortex (PFC), the leader, higher-level-thinking center. It will help to calm your emotional brain, removing some of the fear and uncertainty by creating a feeling of safety with a strategy for support, guidance, and moving forward with your life.

PART TWO
PATH

"I have never climbed Mt. Everest, but I sometimes think it would be easier than navigating the pathway through grief."
— M. Katherine Shear, MD.

5

FINDING A WAY

We all have some understanding of what a labyrinth is. While it's a lot like a maze in its structure, a labyrinth has only one way in and the same way out. Its interconnected pathways can be tangled, perplexing, and shifting. It's easy to feel disoriented: we think we are close to the center of it, only to find ourselves on the perimeter again. Grief is like that. Just when you feel you've made some progress with sorting through this journey, you're triggered by a memory or a holiday, birthday, anniversary, and there you are back in the thick of the emotions, yearning, and numbness. Grief bursts out because grief has no timeline. It flows when it needs to, and this is how it becomes, how it processes...and each process is unique.

My study about the nature of grief didn't begin right after my husband died. How could it? I did want support but support was limited. I attended a few bereavement support groups but couldn't connect. It was as if I was being pushed into a stage, was allowed to rest there for a while, but was encouraged to move to the next stage. Huh? Was I getting grief wrong? The internet was young the year that David died; it was evolving. I didn't find much help or support online. I was on my own with no direction except that I had two children, and I was raising them on my own—a solo parent. I put my attention there and managed to plow through the next several months. Breathe, I told myself, just breathe. I could calm myself down using meditation techniques that were ingrained in my lifestyle. I could put myself into that space of...well...you know the release you feel after you've had a really good cry? That space—the one of not here, not there. Solace. The comfort after a good cry. That shake-yourself-off kind-of feeling. The feeling that tells you that you can pull yourself up, you can take that next step. But it was all a temporary solace that didn't offer the clarity I needed.

We fell into a pattern, my kids and I, an old routine minus David coming home, which oddly wasn't new. David had traveled a lot for his business. He was often away on business trips during the week. It was hard to face that he was never coming home, never, not ever again. That kind of permanence is brutal, and I needed time to sort it out. David was gone but I frequently had dreams of him sitting at the end of our bed telling me he hadn't died and wondering why I had allowed someone to put his obituary in the newspaper. Heartbreaking dreams of my subconscious mind searching for him. This is, in fact, a function of our brains. We've developed neuronal connections to people, pets, and objects that are important to us. We have words, feelings, a life, and plans that are connected to them in our brains. It takes time to consciously understand and process all the implications associated with loss. Susan Anderson, author of *From Abandonment to Healing*, describes this as the "loss of your background object."

With the death of someone we love, our person, comes grief. It's not only their death we're grieving, we're also grieving for ourselves. Our life has been forever changed and we're learning how to navigate all the changes. Our brain is making adjustments and this is important to note. We have innumerable neuronal pathways that link to the person who died, and these pathways don't die with them. Rather, our brain has found this to be somewhat of a distress signal, something that is a concern for our safety—and remember that the brain's main task is to ensure we are safe.

Part of what's happening in this early experience of loss is the brain searching for the person who isn't there anymore. Our brains are going over pathways and connections that have been formed around that person and how that person fit into our lives. It takes time for the brain to adjust. Our safety has been disrupted and our brain is on alert.

Throughout life, we form attachments to people and our brains physically grow strong neuronal connections to them: our parents, grandparents, our siblings and cousins, our children, close friends, and our pets. Most especially someone we've decided to spend the rest of our life with. That person. The one we made plans with and had children with. The one with whom we envisioned a future, aging together, and sharing a curiosity about how our lives would unfold as we achieved our goals.

What does this mean when we're grieving? First, we have all those connections in our brain, some of them shortcuts, linked to our deceased person. The shortcuts could be simple things like our person picks up our children from school on specific days of the week so we can work, or we have a standing date night every week in the city and we need to catch the train at a certain time. It's something that is predictable and we don't have to think about it once it was put in place. We can make adjustments if we need to but it isn't life-changing; it's a pattern, a routine. When we lose someone important to our life, everything changes. Whenever one of the many neuronal pathways associated with that person is triggered by an event, a scent, a sound, a song, or any other thing, our grief-impaired brain searches for our person and uses its energy for that task. Remember that 20% of our body's energy goes to the brain and when we're engaged with higher-level, whole-brain thinking, the PFC uses up most of that energy.

When we lose that anchor person, these neuronal connections to that person don't vanish. Our brains need time to readjust to this changed environment. We've lost our story, our direction, as planned or as spontaneous as it might be. Let's face it, we've lost our world as we know it and we're in the process of creating a new world, a life without our person. And this is going to take time, energy, and tears.

My journey with grief included everything anyone ever wrote about grief. It was also very unique to me. The first two months were settling into the reality that David had died. He was not on another business trip and he would not return home with his triumphs and frustrations. Our children returned to school, I returned to real estate and the other tasks that revolved around keeping our home and lives running. Outwardly we appeared to have settled into a new normal, coping with the tragedy that had befallen us. Home was a different story. Each of us was dealing with David's death in our own way. I was holding it all together for my children. Their emotional stability became my focus. They dealt with their father's death in completely different ways. Ways that were indicative of their connection to him, of their ages, of their developmental growth and understanding. I constantly communicated with teachers, guidance counselors, doctors, and other parents whose children were close to mine. Desperately reaching out for someone to support me, a widow raising two grieving children. I learned as my children processed their grief. I learned not only about their fears for my safety, I learned about my fears for their safety.

6

CHILDREN

"From the day we are born, the brain is literally customizing itself for our own particular lifestyle. The brain naturally prunes away at the cells that aren't being used and stimulated. We want to make sure we are hitting the sounds, the visuals, the motor stimulation so that the child can start life with the optimal number of neural pathways that optimizes their learning and overall mental growth."
— *Shonté Jovan Taylor, The Neuroscientist*

The truest statement about grief is that each person's journey is unique. Children, adolescents, and adults understand and process loss in fundamentally different ways, influenced by their cognitive and emotional developmental stages. My children handled their grief differently, two unique grief journeys encircling their common loss. Not only the loss of a parent (their father in our case) and the intimate relationship they had with him —the shared memories, the personal jokes, the guidance, and love— but also the loss of their sense of safety, financial security, family, their fear that I, their surviving parent, would die and they would be orphaned. There are many secondary losses for children, too. If you choose to move, for a child, this means the loss of their childhood home, their friends, and their school. A child's grief journey affects their developing brain. These effects are a complex interplay of emotional, cognitive, and neurological factors. As neuroscientists learn more about how the brain develops, more thought has been given to how children might developmentally process grief. While research is ongoing, there are some known ways that grief may affect children at various stages of brain development. Take a look at the following list to familiarize yourself with the beauty of a child's blossoming brain and how grief can inhibit its fluency!

EMOTIONAL REGULATION

The brain regions responsible for emotional regulation, such as the prefrontal cortex, are still developing in children. Experiencing grief can present challenges to a child's ability to manage and understand their emotions.

COGNITIVE DEVELOPMENT

Grieving may interfere with concentration, attention, and academic performance, potentially creating a cascade of challenges related to learning and cognition.

STRESS RESPONSE

Grief is often accompanied by elevated levels of stress hormones like cortisol. Chronic exposure to these hormones can impact the developing brain, particularly areas like the hippocampus, which is crucial for memory and stress regulation.

ATTACHMENT AND SOCIAL DEVELOPMENT

Grief can play a significant role in shaping a child's social development and their understanding of relationships. The experience of loss, especially if it involves a parent or primary caregiver, impacts a child's sense of security and attachment. Since attachment patterns are formed early in life, this can have an influence on future relationships.

COPING MECHANISMS

Depending on their age and the support they receive, children may develop various coping mechanisms to deal with grief. These mechanisms can range from healthy expressions of emotion and seeking social support to more detrimental behaviors like withdrawal, denial, or even substance abuse in older children. These coping mechanisms can have lasting effects on both the structure and functioning of the brain.

RESILIENCE AND GROWTH

It's also worth noting that not all effects of experiencing grief early in life are necessarily negative. With the right support, many children develop resilience and emotional intelligence that serves them well later in life. They may become more empathetic, understanding, and mature as a result of coping with loss, which could have positive implications for their social and emotional well-being.

Being aware of the signs of grief in children can help provide them with the emotional and psychological support they might need. Therapy, counseling, and a stable, supportive home environment can mitigate some of the negative neurological and psychological impacts of grief for a child. Given that brain development is an ongoing process extending into early adulthood, the effects of grief can manifest in various ways over time. Therefore, continuous support and monitoring are crucial for helping grieving children navigate the complexities of loss while they are still developing emotionally and cognitively.

We can help our child's growth and health by talking with them, answering their questions, and validating their experience with grief and the strong emotions that accompany it. Children's brains are making connections and developing no matter the circumstances surrounding their lives. Their brains are creating pathways that will influence how they react to and perceive the world around them as adults. The brain is developing rapidly in the first four years of life, processing information from caregivers and the environment. In early childhood, circuitry for learning and association is formed in the memory center of the brain, the hippocampus. Memories that are stored here can create habitual patterns around emotional triggers that can show up as debilitating behaviors in later years.

Children blossom with the novelty of being exposed to fresh ideas and changes in their everyday environment. These kinds of experiences expand their curiosity and help stimulate their brain, increasing neuronal connections. One of the most important things we can do as the surviving parent or caregiver is to allow children to be curious about death and grief, allow them to express their grief through creative activities, art, music, dance, writing, poetry. This is where creating rituals with your children comes into play.

7

RITUALS

Parents and/or caregivers are the pillars of a child's world, providing stability, love, and a sense of normalcy. When one of those pillars is suddenly gone, it's easy for children to feel like their whole world is crumbling. Involving your child in creating some rituals to honor their loss can give them a sense of control over the emotional ride of grief that they're experiencing.

Rituals are like emotional anchors. Whether it's gathering around the table for a family dinner or having a bedtime story read, these small but consistent actions create a sense of order in the chaos that life can sometimes be. And let's be honest, what could be more chaotic and emotionally unsettling for a child than losing a parent or primary caregiver?

Creating rituals allows for a space where emotions can be processed. Grief isn't something that you can just sweep under the rug; it demands to be felt. So having a dedicated time or a series of actions to remember their person can be an emotional outlet. It might be something like lighting a candle every Sunday evening and talking about fond memories or looking through old photos. This not only allows your child to mourn, but also to celebrate the life of their person and keep their memory alive.

Rituals also provide an element of predictability. The world can seem really unpredictable, especially for a grieving child. Having something consistent to hold on to can be very comforting. Whether it's something simple like a nightly bedtime story, sharing a memory about their person, or a more involved monthly visit to their gravesite, it's this repetition that can help instill a sense of control and security and build a new pillar to help stabilize their world.

And let's not forget about connection. Grief can be isolating. Sometimes it feels like you're the only one in the world going through such pain. Rituals can involve other family members, helping children feel connected to a larger support system. This family involvement reassures the child that they are not alone and that it's okay to share their emotions and memories with others who are also grieving.

Rituals can evolve as the child grows. What's comforting and meaningful to a five-year-old might not resonate the same way with that child when they're fifteen. So it's important to keep the lines of communication open and make adjustments as needed.

Rituals can give grieving children something to hold onto when it feels like they're drowning in their emotions. They provide a structured way to mourn, to remember, and to heal. They also offer a sense of stability and connection during a time when both can seem scarce. And that's why they're so vital.

Rituals don't have to be elaborate. They just need to be heartfelt and consistent, offering a reliable way to remember, celebrate, and mourn someone who's no longer around. Sometimes, it's the little things that hold the most meaning.

Here are some events and moments where a ritual could be woven in:

- **Birthday of their person**: A cake, some candles, and maybe a heartfelt letter or drawing that the child can read out loud or keep private. It's a way to celebrate the parent's life rather than just focusing on the loss.
- **Anniversary of their death**: This can be a heavy day, but it could also be an occasion for a special ritual. You could plant a tree, make a perennial garden, or create a memory jar to place little notes about the person in.
- **Holidays**: The first holiday, Hanukkah, Kwanzaa, Christmas, Thanksgiving, or any other significant holiday without that parent is going to be tough. Having a ritual, like hanging a special ornament or lighting a candle, can make space for that parent's presence, even in their absence.
- **Bedtime routine**: Maybe the lost parent used to read bedtime stories. Continuing this in some way, even if it's just reading a favorite story of the deceased parent, can be comforting.
- **Graduations or big milestones**: These are the times kids really wish their parent could be there. A ritual could be wearing a piece of jewelry that belonged to the lost parent or incorporating a photo of them in some creative way.
- **Weekend or monthly outings**: Visiting a place that was special to the deceased parent and the child can make for a comforting ritual. It could be a park, a beach, or even their gravesite.
- **Their person's favorite activity**: Whether it was baseball, painting, or cooking, doing this activity on a regular basis can keep children connected to their parent. It's like sharing a hobby across dimensions.

- **Family dinners**: Maybe the first dinner of every month is dedicated to making the deceased parent's favorite dish. Everyone can share memories as they eat, keeping the focus on joyful remembrance.
- **Watching home videos or looking through photos**: This could be done on a recurring basis, maybe every few months, to remember and discuss the good times.
- **Nightly or weekly conversations**: Setting aside time to openly talk about the lost parent, or even just how the child is feeling, can be a ritual in itself.
- **Saying prayers or reciting poetry**: Whether it's during temple, church, or quietly at home, reciting something meaningful can become a cherished routine.
- **Art projects**: Drawing or crafting something that helps children remember their parent can be both therapeutic and ritualistic. They can add to this "memory project" on significant dates or whenever they feel the need.

Creating a ritual can be incredibly comforting for a child dealing with grief, especially because their young brains are still in the process of learning how to manage complex emotions. As you probably know, a child's brain is like fertile soil—super receptive, but also sensitive. A ritual provides a structured, predictable routine that the developing brain can latch onto, almost like a life raft in an ocean of emotional chaos. This routine helps the brain release feel-good chemicals like dopamine and serotonin, which can act as natural balancers during a time when everything feels off-kilter. Essentially, a ritual can become a cognitive and emotional anchor, giving the child a sense of control and stability amidst the uncontrollable experience of loss.

A COMPREHENSIVE GUIDE FOR UNDERSTANDING A CHILD'S GRIEF

For the sake of time and simplicity, I've created a chart to help you with your child's grief journey. Hopefully, it will give you some insight into their developing brain, how they might experience grief at different ages, and what support they need at each stage in their development to optimize their growing brain.

AGE	BRAIN DEVELOPMENT	GRIEF PROCESS	REACTIVE BEHAVIOR	PROACTIVE SUPPORT	BRAIN AWARENESS
0 - 2	The trillions of brain cells are making connections to caregivers and the environment. Brain "muscle memory" that influences learning develops. Right brain is dominant.	Aware that someone is missing, but no understand-ing of death.	Crying, sleeplessness, anxiety, clinging.	Stable routine, reassurance through touch and meeting physical needs, cuddling.	Forming emotional intelligence through connection with primary caregivers. Social connections. Read to them, play music. Use physical contact, touch, and foods that enhance brain function.
3 - 5	The first four years are crucial to brain development. There's an explosion of connections being made. Brain prunes cells that aren't being stimulated.	Some understanding of death, "magical thinking," asks the same questions.	Behavior might regress, separation anxiety, nightmares, aggressive behavior.	Verbal & physical reassurance, answer questions simply and honestly, listen, love, cuddle.	Read to them; build social connections; vocabulary is developing, so stimulate the brain with music, visuals, physical activity, nutritious food, sleep, hydration.

6 - 9	Between ages 4-7 significant growth of right hemisphere. Right brain is dominant in early childhood. Right brain can feel sensations from the body before we "know" what's going on, processing emotions, creativity, big picture, images, strong nonverbal communication.	Understands that death is forever, questions whether they caused it, might show interest in what happens when someone dies.	Overly protective of surviving parent/ caregiver, exaggerated fears and phobias, health complaints, regression.	Encourage ways to express feelings through art, creativity, music, writing. Involve them in rituals, love, validate feelings, provide reassurance that they are not alone.	Introduce mindfulness practice to help regulate emotions. Journaling, poetry, creative art projects are all mindfulness-inducing practices. Remember touch, hugs are needed, social activities, nutritious food, sleep, hydration, social connections.
10 - 12	Between ages 9-12 significant spike in growth of left hemisphere but right brain is still growing. Between 11-13 nerve fibers are growing between right and left brain hemispheres.	Processing life without their parent who died, struggle with an awareness that death can happen at any time to anyone, realistic view of the finality of death, questions about their care and changes to their family.	Upset by the change in their life, difficulty concentrating, school work suffers, denial, guilt, anxiety, mood swings, nightmares, sleeplessness.	Hold space for them, listen when they want to talk, validate their feelings, find peer support groups for them.	Touch, hugs are important, mindfulness practice. Find activities to stimulate both right & left brain such as playing musical instrument, art, math, science, sports, social activities, nutritional food, sleep, hydration.

13 - 18	Left brain dominates teen years. Logical, rational, verbal, brain is still pruning and sculpting itself. Connectivity and more development of prefrontal cortex ((PFC), higher-order thinking, leader, CEO of brain). Emotions also affect left-brain functions; right brain functioning continues to develop.	Understand the universality of death, might be concerned about their own mortality, want independence but grief holds them back, might hide feelings to "fit in" with peers	Acting out, impulsive and risk behavior, changes to peer group, aggression, anger, physical complaints, defiance, drug/ alcohol use, promiscuity, mood swings	Share feelings with them, encourage expression of their feelings, therapy, peer support group, help with managing feelings	Continue with enriching experiences and activities that stimulate both right & left hemispheres. Allow expression of individuality in safe environments where they can think for themselves, create for themselves. Encourage exercise, nutritious food, sleep, hydration, social connections, mindfulness practice.
19 - 25	The PFC is still developing into the mid 20s. PFC is responsible for judgment, reasoning, planning, impulse control, processing and organizing information.	Understand universality of death, have some degree of independence but have lost an important person in their young life. Feel separate, isolated, disoriented	Can experience prolonged & intense grief. Physical symptoms, mental anguish, feeling that life has been interrupted, guilt, anger, feeling detached, loss of appetite, unable to deal with life's challenges, finding relief with drug & alcohol use	Help them find resources to fall back on. Young adult grief support groups. Hold space and listen to their fears and worries. Help with decision making.	Develop an awareness of how the brain processes grief and how negative habits can influence dopamine release that will affect adult life. Nutritious food, sleep, hydration, social connections, and mindfulness practice.

> Moving my family to Vermont became my raft in the turbulent waters I was navigating. I gathered my children and set out to move. A total flight plan. I needed to keep my family safe and, in my mind, East Hampton had become unsafe, plus, I thought I had no other options. Looking back, I did have other options. I had several alternatives to moving to Vermont, but at the time, I couldn't see them. My emotional brain was navigating. I was in an emergency state of mind, an "amygdala hijack." I didn't have the presence of mind, the power of my executive functioning brain, to question or deeply look into how this choice was going to play out. I couldn't figure out the questions to ask myself and I knew that no one in my family or circle of friends understood the gravity of how I felt.

"amygdala hijack"[1]

8

MISTAKE #2:
FLIGHT

G rief is a slippery slope and it only takes one incident to send you to the bottom of the proverbial barrel and that, my dears, is where we were—the muck at the bottom of the barrel. You know that feeling when you realize how fragile the veneer of pretense is? Was I pretending we were doing okay? What had I missed? Why hadn't this come with instructions? But grief has no manual, it has no set course. I needed tangible help and support. I needed the structure to know what to ask for. It was all so overwhelming and here I was. I had arrived at the bottom of the barrel, spiraling in my own abyss, and the way out was flight. I didn't have any counsel but my own. I suppose you can say I felt totally alone, not understood, afraid, and pushed to implement the decision that had already been made by all of us. A path of least resistance. Vermont.

This was the first life-changing decision that I decided to make and, be aware dear reader, the first life-changing decision you have to make after losing someone is hard. I had no one I could talk to rationally about this completely emotional decision I was making—after all I didn't have a Board of Trust-eds! A few friends questioned me about what I was doing and why Vermont, but *this was the decision we had made as a family the month before David died.* It became my lifeline, my raft in this turbulence, my only option. Move to Vermont. Even though David and I had formed many deep connections with our local friends and had started an East Hampton meditation group that was gaining traction, I longed for the larger Buddhist community in Vermont where I thought I would find more support for myself, a safe place for me to grieve and practice meditation. The funny thing about where we lived now was that I was supporting most of the friends who stopped by to check in on me. They were also grieving David's death. They came to my house to let it out, to cry. I consoled them. They told me how strong I was. We hugged. They left. They had closure. I wanted that and I thought I could find it away from East Hampton. We moved to Vermont less than a year after David had died even though I had made a pledge to myself to stay put for at least the first two years of my widowhood. My mind was clouded by the emotional turmoil of grief along with the fear about my children's safety, and I was haunted by one of the main reasons David and I made the "Move to Vermont" decision: high school. Now I saw this move as my only option, the option that would keep my family safe.

Major mistake, and a decision made strictly through emotions and brain fog. When we're grieving, most of the energy that our brain uses is being hijacked by our limbic system, our emotional brain, which leaves very little energy for our executive brain's involvement in the decision-making process. We're essentially being hijacked by our amygdala and limbic system—the emotional center of our brain.

The "amygdala hijack" is a term coined by psychologist and author Daniel Goleman to describe those moments when your emotions completely overrule your rational thinking. Ever snapped at someone when you were stressed and thought, "Why did I just do that?" That's your amygdala hijacking you, your limbic system taking control.

So, let's break it down. The amygdala is a small almond-shaped cluster of nuclei in your brain. It's like your emotional processing center, and it is responsible for triggering strong emotional responses like fear and aggression. The amygdala is a busy little part of the brain, and it doesn't limit itself to just fear and aggression. It plays a role in a wide range of emotions, including pleasure, sadness, and even love. Now, usually, your brain does a good job of balancing emotion with rational thought. When you encounter something that stirs up emotions, that information typically goes through the prefrontal cortex (PFC), the CEO of your brain. The PFC evaluates the situation, considers the pros and cons, and then helps decide how to react.

But sometimes, especially when we're stressed or threatened, the amygdala doesn't wait for our rational brain to chime in. It just takes over and goes, "I got this!" Except it doesn't "got this" in a way that you'd like. It reacts quickly and forcefully, pushing you into a "fight, flight, freeze, or fawn" response before you've had a chance to think things through.

In an amygdala hijack we go "limbic"; we have strong emotional reactions that can feel entirely disproportionate to the situation at hand. When you're grieving, your emotional state is often height-ened, making you more susceptible to intense and sometimes unpredictable reactions. You might find yourself snapping at people, breaking down in tears at the slightest trigger, or even freezing up when faced with seemingly simple decisions. That's your amygdala trying to handle the potent mix of sadness, loss, anger, and perhaps even guilt, sometimes bypassing your rational brain in the process. Recognizing that you may be more prone to amygdala hijacks while grieving can be a first step in managing your reactions and finding more balanced ways to cope with your emotions. These are times when emotions don't just tip the scale but completely knock reason and logic off it. Once you know what it is, you can start to recognize the signs and maybe, just maybe, give your rational mind time to catch up and take control of the situation. Take a deep breath, count to ten, and give your whole brain a chance to weigh in.

My world had fallen apart and I was on my own to put it back together. At some point, this became unrealistic, and I am the first to admit that. My flight from East Hampton to Vermont was my attempt to get the support and care I needed while grieving the tremendous loss of David in my life. I was very aware that I needed help processing the different emotions, fears, and insecurities that his death triggered, both for myself and my children. I wasn't prepared for the flood of emotions that were unleashed as I prepared for the move and sale of our family home and the car David had bought me for our tenth wedding anniversary: a 1974 BMW 2002. As fate would have it, the man who bought this car became my lover, business partner, and demise. The repercussions of that first encounter set my life and the lives of my children into a Tasmanian whirlwind of chaos and pain in addition to processing our grief. It is my cautionary tale for your well-being and in my grief journey—it was Mistake #3.

9

MISTAKE #3:
RELATIONSHIP

Most of the days after my husband's death were clouded by brain fog. I remember getting up, stumbling through our morning routine, getting my kids to school, and coming back to a house that he no longer was a part of. His presence, his office, and all of his "things" were still there, but physically, he was gone. As I navigated my grief, there came a point where I felt this surprising sense of freedom from the constraints of having a husband. Crazy, right? I remember the day I actually sat on my bed, threw my arms up and shouted "I'm free!" I was free of the traditional, domestic role I had fallen into after our children were born. One of those ingrained throwbacks defining the roles of women and men—you know, the breadwinner and the domestic goddess. As much as our marriage was a product of the free love, free your mind, hippie, baby boomer generation, there were still struggles defining our roles. Did you find that in your relationship? If so, don't shy away from admitting that something was released when your partner passed. Maybe something you argued about or how something made you feel taken advantage of. Don't feel guilty about admitting the deficiencies in your relationship with your deceased partner. It does not serve you to do that. Don't turn them into someone who didn't have any flaws, flaws that affected you. Understanding that it wasn't always perfect, yet deeply valuing what you shared, is all part of your grief journey.

I'm going to be really honest right now. My marriage wasn't some sort of fairy tale; it had its good moments and its bad, its bumps and its smooth stretches. It had its ups and downs, its rocky ledges and clear blue skies. When my husband died, we were in one of those clear blue sky times. We had re-discovered one another all over again—saw what made us click in the first place and how we had grown and evolved in our time together. We had both changed, gaining the compassionate compromise that relationships require. This last change, his death, was and is hard to deal with.

The days blurred into one another, I was looking for purpose and everything felt empty. Until one day, I took stock of myself and told myself that my one purpose was to raise my two children. Period. Keep them safe, keep them healthy, hug them and love them. I did not want nor was I looking to get into another relationship with another man. Almost everyone who has lost their life partner, whether it be through death, divorce, or leaving an abusive relation-ship, has probably heard the term "my chapter two." It refers to finding another partner. Not someone to replace the person we lost, but someone to evolve with, to find a new way with. I wasn't at all ready for that, it would take years, I thought. But my situation felt desperate. The staid advice of "don't do anything for the first year" was unraveling for me. I had to do **something**. I had to protect my children from all sorts of things that ticked my worry boxes. I was pushed over the edge and grasping for the ring on a parachute. I desperately wanted help and with a desperation that coursed through my body, mind, and spirit, I called out to the universe from the very depths of desire, I called so deeply that the universe had nothing else to do but follow my command. Because that's what it was: a command. I told the universe to bring me a man. I wanted a boyfriend just like my girlfriend's new boyfriend. That is what I yelled out. "Help me. Help me. Help me get out of this. Send me someone who will keep me safe, who will be a partner." "Who will walk beside me and comfort my freaked-outness."

10

BE CAREFUL WHAT YOU ASK FOR

T wo weeks before our move to Vermont, I decided to sell the sweet car my husband had given me as a gift for our tenth wedding anniversary. It was a 1974 BMW, 2002 model, white exterior, navy blue leather interior, stick shift, 2-door, Hampton's fun-mobile, and, sadly, it would not do well on the dirt roads and hills of Vermont. I asked a friend who lived on a well-traveled road in the Village of East Hampton if I could put it on her lawn so people would see that it was for sale. It was a prime location and, as it turned out, one of the people who called me about purchasing the car was someone my girlfriend knew. We struck up a deal and, with a sigh of relief, I checked off "sell the BMW" from my list and arranged for the buyer to call me and pick it up from my house after the weekend.

It was July 4th weekend. The first July 4th since my husband's death. We were moving the following week. Packing up my house. Giving things away. Crying and very vulnerable. The weekend was almost over. I hadn't heard from this interested (though my first impression was crazy) buyer for my car, but he had left his phone number, so I called. I left a message letting him know I was moving the upcoming week and that if he was still interested in the car he had to call me immediately or it was going back on my friend's lawn. I had no time to be jerked around.

II

AN UNEXPECTED "CHAPTER TWO" AND A WOLF AT MY DOOR

T he following day, he showed up in my driveway exclaiming "you're moving?!!" His words hit my grief wall, broke through and within seconds the tears were flowing. This man, who I didn't know at all, showed the empathy and concern that I so desperately longed for. We sat on the porch stairs and talked for hours. He comforted me and my judgment of him changed. He was kind and took the time from his workday to sit and talk with me. He had shown up. He would bring me the money for the car the next day.

He unexpectedly came back later that afternoon with a proposition to help me out of the dilemma I had created for myself around my house. I listened and was hooked, not really by his plan (which, in retrospect, was all about serving his needs at my expense), but because he wanted to help me. He wanted to be a shoulder for me. I walked him to the driveway and went to give him a hug. He backed off, extended his hand and we shook hands. The deal was sealed. He was a gift, the universe had answered! He was an answer to some of the worries I had about leaving my house in East Hampton unattended while moving to and living in another state. I wasn't sure if I was going to rent my East Hampton house or sell it. He offered to rent it from me and do some renovations to enhance it. I was okay with that. It was a shortcut leading to an irrational decision. Remember, I had no support network. I was alone. I guess my friends and family saw me as independent and able to carry on, make decisions, and take care of my children. Believe me, this wasn't the case. Enter a man, seemingly strong, charismatic, and offering to help me when I was forgotten by everyone else in my life. I couldn't help but to jump at his offer. I ignored my gut instinct and first impression of "this guy is crazy." Help. Someone wanted to help. Buying my car and wanting to help. It was a sign from the heavens. A gift. A friend. A big mistake.

I had no one that I trusted checking in on me. No Board of Trusteds, and that kind of counsel is important. I was operating strictly from my limbic system.

High on that feeling of "falling in love," I suddenly found myself in a hot relationship with the man who bought my car. As my mind indulged in this romantic fantasy, he moved into my home in East Hampton with the illusion of paying rent to offset my costs and making some improvements to help bolster its inevitable sale. All of this happened within days of my move to Vermont. As my children and I settled into our new home, I began a long-distance romance of late, late-night two-to-three-hour phone calls with this man that left me depleted during the day. But again, I was high on that feeling of "falling in love." It wasn't anything I was ready for, but I created a romantic fantasy around it. The universe had responded to my command! This man fulfilled a romantic fantasy I had about being in love with a man from another country, who spoke another language, and who wanted only me.

Within a year, my East Hampton house was sold and he moved into my house in Vermont. From the time we loaded up the truck with the remaining contents of my East Hampton house, his attitude changed. He started being verbally brutish to my son. I had no uncertainty letting him know about how unacceptable his behavior was. Thinking this was caused by the tension of moving, I gave him some leeway. I spoke to him calmly and as rationally as my grieving brain could muster. But the true nature and the reality of who this man truly was had presented itself. A cunning, narcissistic, psychologically and emotionally abusive man who I had let into my children's lives, and during that year, had started a business with. He diminished our grief about David and, although I tried to reason with him, the same battle was fought over and over again. Although he acknowledged my words and my concern, things only got worse as the weeks and months passed. Less than a year later, those feel-good neurochemicals I was high on had dissipated, the "fantasies" had played themselves out and I felt I was stuck. Stuck in an unwanted relationship with a narcissistic sociopath who I had started a business with. I felt embarrassed and ashamed. I had been isolated by him and abandoned by friends, my community in Vermont, because of their dislike for him. I was in a state of turmoil on top of turmoil. Once again, with no one to turn to, I held my own council. A drowning woman, grasping at straws, constantly being pushed under by someone who she had let into her life because she thought he was safe.

> ## Gut Feeling
>
> Some of the most successful people out there swear by trusting their instincts. They make it sound like some sort of mystical power but, really, it's a skill you can develop over time. It starts with listening to yourself, becoming attuned to those gut feelings, and then actually acting on them to see what happens. You'll probably find that the more you trust your intuition, the more accurate and useful it becomes. The next time you're faced with a decision and your gut is trying to tell you something, give it a listen. It doesn't mean you have to throw logic and reasoning out the window, but a little intuitive nudge could be the tiebreaker you need to make the best choice for you.

12

MISTAKE #4:
NOT HONORING MY INTUITION

My brain was on fire with the chemicals of love; I wanted this man. He had a magnetic, charismatic energy. In the beginning, he was gentle and kind to my kids, and I envisioned a future that was loving and prosperous for all of us. Allowing someone I didn't know to move into my former home that was hundreds of miles from where I now lived equaled commitment to my grieving brain. The reality was that red flags had begun to wave and I blissfully ignored all of them, wanting my version of this new relationship to be true. But sometimes you've just got to trust that little voice inside you, or that uneasy feeling in your stomach that says, "Hmm, maybe don't go down that path."

Think about it. Our brains are these incredibly complex machines, processing tons of information every second, much of which we're not even consciously aware of. Your gut feeling is like your brain's way of sending you a text message saying, "Hey, I've processed all this data behind the scenes and you might want to pay attention to this."

Have you ever met someone and you couldn't put your finger on it, but something felt off? Or maybe you've contemplated a job offer, and on paper it looked amazing, but something was just nagging at you? That's your intuition talking. It might be your brain picking up on subtle signals like body language, or maybe it's drawing on past experiences that you haven't even thought about in years.

Now, that's not to say you should just blindly follow your gut every time. If your gut's telling you to eat a third slice of cake, maybe second-guess that one. But when it comes to bigger life choices or even smaller daily interactions, your intuition is like your built-in GPS. It's been calibrated over years and years of experiences, relationships, triumphs, and mistakes. Ignoring it is like driving past a stop sign just because your map didn't mark it.

As for grief and new romance—it's like mixing fire and water, isn't it? Both are intense, both can be consuming, and they often don't play well together. When we're grieving, all kinds of emotions are swirling around, and it can be hard to make sense of what you're actually feeling. And that's where the gut feelings become especially important, yet also complicated.

When you've lost someone you love, or you're going through a serious breakup or divorce, your emotional state is all over the place. You know that feeling, the one where you're walking through a dense fog then, out of the blue, someone new steps into your life and suddenly there's this potential for romance. On the surface, it feels like a breath of fresh air, a distraction, maybe even a lifeline. But deep down, your gut is waving red flags like it's trying to signal a ship lost at sea.

Ignoring that gut reaction is tempting. Oh boy, is it tempting! Because the heart wants what it wants, right? And when you're grieving, sometimes you're desperate for anything that will make you feel better, even for a moment. But your intuition is still there, trying to break through the emotional noise to tell you, "Hey, something's not quite right here."

That gut feeling could be your subconscious reminding you that you're emotionally vulnerable, and that you might not be seeing the situation or the new person clearly. Or maybe it's recognizing patterns that you've fallen into before and trying to help you steer clear this time. It's like a protective friend who sees you about to make the same mistake again and tugs you back, even when you think you want to move forward.

In the throes of grief, it's so easy to sweep those intuitive nudges under the rug. Because, let's face it, grief sucks. It's one of the hardest things you'll ever go through, and the idea that someone new could make it even a tiny bit easier is incredibly seductive. But it's also risky to make big emotional investments when you're already carrying so much emotional debt.

So, what do you do? Take a step back, and give yourself a moment to listen to that gut feeling. It doesn't mean you have to cut ties with the new romantic interest immediately, but perhaps slow down a bit. Use the time to reflect, to check in with yourself, to even talk it through with a trusted member of your board, or your therapist. Balancing intuition with conscious thought could give you the perspective you need to make a healthier choice for yourself.

Remember, grief has a way of distorting the lens through which we view the world, including new relationships. But your gut feeling is your built-in autofocus trying to correct the image. It's not fool-proof, but it's often worth listening to.

> My fear of leaving the relationship centered around the business we had started together. I had become financially entwined with him. It wasn't just a romantic relationship gone sour—we were business partners. I had started a business with him and it was my money that was funding all of it. Any promises he had made about work and support were words without substance. He wouldn't give an inch, and I kept moving the line of my principles. I spent seven years trying to understand and accommodate this man, to no avail. It seriously compromised me, my grieving experience, and my children's grieving. It was toxic. Do not be afraid to leave a relationship if there isn't respect for your process.

13

MISTAKE #5:
FINANCIAL RESPONSIBILITY

I was fraught with the weight of difficult decisions when he came into our lives. He was buying a car from me—a car my husband had bought as a present for our 10th wedding anniversary. He came at one of the most vulnerable times of my life and offered a shoulder to lean on. A rock to rest on. A rock for a rock to rest on because I had become the rock for so many people in my life. My children, of course. My late husband's parents as he was an only child and they were devastated. Losing a child is the ultimate devastation for a parent, and I could not and cannot fathom the depth of the pain, torment, and grief that goes with it. My parents, who were concerned for my well-being and my ability to care for myself and my children. Our friends, both near and far, many of whom were deep in their own grief over the tragic death of David, who had been their friend, meditation instructor, teacher, community leader, volunteer fireman, businessman, entrepreneurial strategist, and genius. So many of whom came to **me** for solace even though I was the widow.

We were left financially secure, my children and me. Having enough money to pay the bills was one thing I didn't need to concern myself with in the immediate future. At least that's what I thought. David had been our financial planner and though we had talked about finding a certified financial planner, we hadn't done anything about it. Several friends stepped in to help—none of them financial planners, all of them wanting me to set up an account with their investment firms. I am a strong person, a resilient woman, independent, subject to the errors of my own counsel. I still have a lot to learn and a long way to go to bring it all together, if all together is a thing that anyone can accomplish. There were a lot of life experiences, from childhood through adulthood, that gave me my strength and independence. My not trusting certain ways of life over others. Some kind of jaded clear-seeing of what I didn't want. I had worked on Wall Street, and I didn't trust that my money would be safe there. In fact, meeting with these investment bankers and hearing what they had to say about the amount of money I had and what my future looked like increased the anxiety I already had about every other aspect of life without David.

Since I had been swept off my feet by this Chapter Two man and ignored the red flags and my gut reactions, when we decided to start a business together, I felt confident about the outcome and my ability to create financial stability and wealth for my children, for our future. Sadly, once a sociopath enters your life, all bets are off. The business we started, the life we began together checked off a lot of things on my bucket list: renovate old buildings, live in a big house, own horses. It was devastating when the bubble popped and these dreams turned into nightmares. You might ask why I endured this, why I didn't throw him out. The simple answer is I was tied to him financially through the business we had started together. The financial well-being of my family was at stake. It was all my money, and all the debt was in my name. There were projects that were started that he needed to finish, or so I reasoned. I was the cash equity; he was the sweat equity. The critical decisions I made in the first two years after my husband's death created an unsteady foundation for moving forward, and my grieving mind couldn't see a way to sort out the situation. In the end, sticking with it, with the determination to see it through, to have him finish the projects and then dissolve the company was another bad decision.

I can't stress enough how you must have the counsel of an objective Board of Trust-eds. People you trust to help you organize and plan your life forward. There's an old adage that applies here: putting two heads together, two brains working on something simultaneously, creates a third more powerful brain. Take time to grieve, but also take time to work on a life plan with your Board of Trust-eds.

14

CREATING A LIFE PLAN,
STARTING WITH YOU

Chapter 2 of your life is totally, 100% about Y.O.U. I cannot emphasize that enough. Chapter 2 = YOU. So take time and make an assessment of yourself. As you work on redefining your journey and setting a new direction, this form of introspection can offer fresh perspectives on your personal dynamics. It hinges on that timeless question pondered by humanity since the dawn of consciousness: "Who am I?" This is a query you'll need to address in your present situation. While it may seem like a philosophical or even mystical question, it's also a practical one that can guide you as you navigate the intricate maze of loss, grief, and mourning. This reflective exercise can offer a respite from the emotional whirlwind that seems to spin uncontrollably, guiding you toward more stable footing. You know what I'm saying, right? We've subconsciously defined ourselves and our life path as part of something, whether it's a relationship, career, title or where we live. When a life-altering change happens, we find our identity isn't as fixed as we once believed. Life-altering changes can function as mirrors, reflecting back to us the components of our lives that we were perhaps too preoccupied to notice. The death of our person is a big shift. It's the end of a long-term relationship, a change in social standing. It could mean a career upheaval, or we might need to make a significant move. These kinds of changes often shatter the boxes we've put ourselves in. Suddenly, we find that we are not just a spouse, an executive, a "city person," or a "suburban mom." We are complex beings with multifaceted identities, capable of adaptation, growth, and transformation.

Life-altering changes force us to reassess the narratives we've constructed about ourselves. These narratives may be limiting or empowering, but either way, they shape our actions, our world-views, and even our self-worth. When these narratives are upended, it can be disorienting, but it is also an opportunity for growth. We can choose to see these changes as a kind of shedding—a chance to let go of the aspects of ourselves that no longer serve us and to embrace new roles, relationships, and experiences that align with our core values and aspirations.

Ultimately, these changes remind us that our identities are works in progress, rather than completed manuscripts. While disentangling our sense of self from external markers can be a difficult process, it can also be incredibly liberating. When we understand that our worth isn't tied to any single aspect of our lives, we free ourselves to explore new opportunities, to build more authentic relationships, and to carve out a life path that reflects not just societal expectations or familiar routines, but our deepest, most authentic selves.

WHO AM I?

So, how do we begin to answer that question? I've found that a useful approach to exploring the question "Who am I?" is to create a table with multiple titled columns. To get you started, here are a few of the column headings I've used:

"Cosmic Identity": Start with a more ethereal or spiritual perspective if that resonates with you. You might title this column "I am a child of the universe..." Dive into your interconnectedness with all things, your spiritual leanings, or a broader cosmic sense of self.

"Childhood Self": Label this column "Who I saw myself to be as a child." Think back to your early years, your dreams, and your self-perceptions during that innocent time. What did you want to be when you grew up? What were your likes and dislikes?

"Adolescent Evolution": Title this "Who I came to be in my youth." Consider the transformational teenage years and early adulthood. What were your aspirations, your struggles, your triumphs? How did your sense of identity shift?

"The Relational Self": This one could be called "Who I defined myself to be in my relationship." Reflect on your partnership, how it influenced your identity, and the roles you took on. This could include everything from emotional roles to practical chores.

"The Mourner's Identity": Name this column "Who I am right now, as a mourner." This is the raw, present self—steeped in grief but also in the potential for new understanding and growth. What aspects of your identity have come to the forefront since your loss?

Intersections and Commonalities: After filling out the columns, take a moment to observe where these different visions of "Self" intersect. What is the common thread running through these varying stages or perspectives?

I understand you're navigating through the foggy labyrinth of grief, and your brain isn't functioning at its best. But remember, it's important not to judge what comes up as you do this exercise. Rather, let the exercise serve as a tool for introspection, however murky or unclear the insights might initially appear.

SELF DISCOVERY

Navigating the loss of a spouse or life partner, your person, is an emotional and transformative journey, one that requires us to reassess not just who we were, but who we'll become in this new chapter of life. This shift isn't just about accepting what's happened; it's also about becoming aware of your own identity outside the context of your marriage or relationship.

Now that you've pondered and have some insight into who you were and are, the next step is to delve deeper into this process of self-discovery. You can start by setting aside some quiet time with a notebook or computer. Reflect on the roles you played within the relationship. Were you the financial planner, the organizer, the caretaker? Think about the domestic chores you shared and the reasons behind your lifestyle choices. Why did you live in a certain place? Was it a mutual decision?

As you think about these questions, also consider the responsibilities that your person took on, tasks and roles that now rest solely on your shoulders.

The more you explore these facets of your life, diving into both conscious and subconscious aspects, the better equipped you'll be to make thoughtful decisions about your future. By doing this deep internal work, you can develop a more comprehensive plan, one that not only meets your logistical needs but also nurtures emotional peace and balance for the years ahead.

To engage deeply with this exploration, here's a reflective exercise that can help illuminate your path forward, revealing opportunities that may be quietly bubbling in your consciousness. This process is akin to collecting scattered pieces of a puzzle and tentatively laying out a new path, even if it's temporary for now. So, grab a journal, paper and pen, and ponder the following questions:

What defined you before your life intertwined with your love? Where were you before? What were you doing? What was occupying your time and attention?

Did you have a mental list of subjects or skills you wanted to explore? If so, what were they?

Sketch a portrait of yourself during that period—your pursuits, ambitions, and interests. What dreams fueled your spirit? Where did you envision your life heading? What captivated your curiosity or passion?

By revisiting the person you were before you entered your relationship, you're not just reminiscing; you're recalibrating your compass for the journey ahead. This exercise allows you to align your present self with your past dreams and curiosities, offering a fresh perspective on your evolving path.

Look at who you were before your relationship with your person. Look at who you became. What changed? Did the direction of your life change because of meeting and falling in love with your person? How? Why? Look at who you are because of meeting, loving, and creating a life with them. Look at who you are after witnessing their death. Write about these contemplations. Not only will this help you navigate your grief, but it also directs your brain's energy to the prefrontal cortex and away from your limbic system. You are in charge. Think of it like shifting into drive. You can consciously engage both your right and left hemispheres. Be analytical and be creative about these questions. Maybe one of them prompts you to create a mind map, a vision board, or write a poem. Or perhaps you need to make a business plan for your life, have strategies, weekly planning and accountability with your Board of Trust-eds.

When we encounter love, our bodies and minds undergo a kind of alchemy. Elevated by dopamine—the brain's "feel-good" neuro-transmitter—we often find ourselves in a euphoric state, acting on impulse rather than reason. Falling in love is an effortless, instanta-neous experience, buoyed by these intoxicating neurochemicals. However, this heady state has its drawbacks: it can cloud our judg-ment, sideline our intuition, and muffle the voice of our rational selves. We might minimize imperfections or even shift our personal boundaries to accommodate this new infatuation.

This is why initially choosing yourself as your "Chapter 2" and making yourself your first priority is so crucial. In the aftermath of profound loss, the clarity you gain by pausing and reflecting on your own needs and boundaries becomes invaluable. It's an opportunity to recalibrate, to see yourself outside the haze of a dopamine-fueled second chapter and make decisions based on a more balanced, self-aware perspective. Through this introspection, you can create a pathway that honors not just the love you had, but also the person you are—and the person you wish to become. Knowing yourself enough to ask the right questions will keep you from more heart-break. A genuine, true loving long-term relationship takes effort in the best of times. Give yourself time to make that relationship with yourself and "date" yourself first![1]. Once you have that self-aware-ness, you can feel confident about opening yourself to dating other people again.

EMOTIONAL ANCHORS

Embarking on a journey of self-discovery is challenging even in the best of times, let alone when grappling with the emotional mael-strom of grief. Yet, it's precisely in these trying moments that certain activities can act as emotional anchors. Our brains crave certainty, and one way to provide this is through goal setting—a concept that might feel completely alien when you're counting it a victory just to get dressed and step outside.

Yes, the notion of setting goals may seem incongruous during the initial stages of grief. However, goal setting operates on various psychological levels. When you give yourself a tangible task, it can help to disengage the amygdala—the part of the brain responsible for emotional responses and our innate "fight or flight" reactions. Your amygdala wants to protect you; it craves the certainty that your world, now shattered by the loss of your loved one, can no longer provide.

Setting even small goals can make a big difference. Perhaps it's dedicating ten minutes to journaling while savoring a cup of tea or coffee. It could also be as simple as planning a week's menu full of brain-boosting foods, compiling a shopping list, and then making a trip to the grocery store. These types of tasks engage higher cognitive functions, drawing you into a state of mindful focus.

Here's the remarkable part: accomplishing these small tasks releases dopamine, the same "feel-good" neurotransmitter that comes into play when you fall in love. Achieving these simple goals not only gives you a sense of accomplishment, but also biochemically eases your emotional turmoil, at least temporarily.

So, take a moment to jot down three small goals or tasks you'd like to accomplish. Whether you use traditional pen and paper—which many find most effective—or your electronic device of choice, this exercise could serve you well. Personally, I've found that setting these goals during the evening or nighttime sets a constructive tone for the days ahead, providing a sense of purpose and, yes, a touch of much-needed certainty.

When I implemented this approach, I found that waking up to a new day carried with it a hint of certainty, a subtle but impactful shift. If I felt myself spiraling into emotional turmoil again, the simple act of taking out my pen and paper to set another goal for the upcoming hours served as an anchor. When grief feels all-encompassing, penning a plan—even for just the next hour or two—offers a concrete focus, giving your brain the certainty it yearns for, and a momentary respite from emotional turbulence.

But the benefits go deeper. Your brain is constantly processing—much of it below the threshold of conscious thought. When you set a goal, even a modest one, it engages not only your conscious mind but also your subconscious cognitive machinery. Your ability to both process grief and conceive a path forward is aided by this mental roadmap. Your brain will, whether you're fully aware of it or not, guide you towards the goals you've set. This introduces a sense of safety; our brains are hardwired to equate certainty with security.

This is one reason why change—particularly the transformative, irrevocable change wrought by the loss of a loved one—is so jarring. Our instincts crave permanence in an impermanent world. By setting goals, even small ones, you're providing your emotional and cognitive systems with a modicum of that elusive quality: certainty. It's not a panacea for the complexities of grief, but it's a step—sometimes a crucial one—toward navigating through it.

First, find you—rediscover who you are, and from there, be discerning about your direction—no matter how temporary that direction might feel. Remember, you don't have to navigate this journey alone. You have the counsel of your Board of Trust-eds to bounce ideas off and share your reflections and the insights you've gleaned about yourself. This is about assembling the tapestry of your identity, mapping out your desires and needs with as much clarity as you can muster in this emotionally laden time.

Why does this task feel so insurmountable? Because, in our hearts, we long for the return of the ones we've lost. We yearn for their presence, their unique blend of virtues and imperfections. We miss the minor irritations as much as the major joys—perhaps even fantasizing about hearing that same old joke one more time. The desire to reverse time can become an overwhelming preoccupation. This is understandable; the emotional pull is profoundly human.

Change is invariably difficult, and the death of a life partner is one of the most excruciating forms of change imaginable. You are a beautiful, remarkable being who has endured a devastating upheaval, a change that tests the very limits of emotional resilience. Your heart may feel as if it's been stretched to breaking, and I am right there with you in acknowledging the raw pain of that experience. This is the unforgiving lesson of impermanence, one that strips away all illusions and exposes our most vulnerable selves.

PART THREE
FINDING RESILIENCE

15

CREATING A LIFE PLAN
WHOLE-BRAIN THINKING

Whole-brain thinking is a holistic approach to cognition and problem solving that seeks to integrate both the analytical and creative sides of your mind. Traditional thought often segregates our mental faculties into two hemispheres—the left, known for its logical, structured thinking, and the right, celebrated for its creativity and emotional intelligence. Whole-brain thinking aims to marry these seemingly disparate elements into a unified cognitive experience.

In the realm of practicality, this means activating your logical faculties when making plans, analyzing problems, or sequencing tasks, while also tapping into your intuitive and emotional sides to understand nuance, interpret feelings, and generate creative solutions. By balancing these aspects, you're better equipped to navigate the complex array of challenges that life—particularly a life undergoing significant change—throws your way.

Why does this matter, especially now, as you grapple with such transformative and traumatic life events? Well, grief tends to unmoor us, destabilizing the delicate balance between reason and emotion. During times of profound loss, your emotional brain—the

93

limbic system—might be in overdrive, making it difficult to think clearly or make rational choices. On the other hand, retreating too far into analytical thought could detach you from the vital emotional processing that processing grief requires.

By embracing whole-brain thinking, you stand a better chance of maintaining equilibrium during this emotionally volatile period. You could apply logical strategies to cope with the immediate tasks at hand, such as dealing with financial matters or planning memorial services. At the same time, you can honor your emotions, allowing them the space to breathe, enabling you to adapt and evolve—even in the face of life's most challenging tribulations, like the landscape of grief you're currently navigating.

Since whole-brain thinking is all about leveraging the full spectrum of your mental capabilities, brain dumps and mind maps *(See appendix 5)* are the dynamic duo for getting started. A brain dump lets you unload everything in your head without judging or categorizing, tapping into your free-flowing, creative right brain. Once you've emptied the mental cache, you can switch gears to your more analytical left brain and use a mind map to structure those thoughts, find connections, and create a game plan. So you're essentially getting the best of both worlds—free-form creativity and structured analysis. Using brain dumps and mind maps together for whole-brain thinking is like having a mental toolbox, stocked with just the right tools for any kind of cognitive job. Whether you need the free-wheeling creativity of a paintbrush (that's your brain dump) or the precision of a measuring tape (your mind map), you've got what you need to think things through in a balanced and comprehensive way.

16

A GRIEVER'S GUIDE TO THE WHEEL OF LIFE

Navigating the emotional quagmire of grief is far from a straightforward journey; it's more like a twisting labyrinth that requires all of your senses to traverse. This is where the "Wheel of Life" concept taken from a life coach's toolbox can provide a structured yet flexible framework. When seen through the lens of whole-brain thinking and adapted for the grieving process, this tool can be both a map and a compass as you find your way through this heart-wrenching chapter of your life.

COMPONENTS OF THE GRIEVING WHEEL OF LIFE

- **Emotional Well-Being:** This is where you give yourself permission to feel. Grieving is a messy, unpredictable process; be patient with yourself. Engage both your emotional and rational brain to acknowledge, label, and understand your feelings. This is the space to honor your emotions without judgment.

- **Physical Health:** Grief takes a toll on the body. Your logical brain will help you remember the practical things —eating, sleeping, exercising—while your emotional brain will remind you to be gentle with yourself. Grieving exhausts the body. Your analytical mind helps you take care of the basics—nutrition, sleep, physical activity—while your intuitive brain reminds you to exercise self-compassion.
- **Relationships/Family:** Social connections. Striking the right balance is crucial. Use your rational mind to establish healthy boundaries and your emotional brain to stay receptive to love and support from others.
- **Career/Work:** Grieving doesn't pause for a job. It doesn't follow a schedule, nor can you leave it at the door of your office or place of employment. This is where your rational brain can help you manage tasks and decide if and when to return to work, while your emotional brain helps you gauge what you're really up for, your readiness to cope with your work life.
- **Finances:** Dealing with numbers and budgets may seem overwhelming during this time, but it's a necessary requirement. Your logical brain tackles the numbers for your budget, while your emotional side helps you align your spending with what truly supports your well-being.
- **Personal Development:** With grief, your identity shifts. This is an opportunity to reflect on, "Who am I now?" "Who have I become?" Engage in activities, books, hobbies or courses that feel enriching.
- **Spiritual Insight:** This is often where the deepest questions arise, as you ponder the existential "whys" and "what-ifs." Balancing ritualized religious practices with intuitive spiritual exploration offers a comprehensive approach.

- **Leisure/Recreation/Joy**: Although it may seem trivial now, fun is a part of life and well-being. Your rational brain will tell you to take a break, while your emotional side will help you find activities that genuinely uplift you.

CREATING YOUR WHOLE-BRAIN GRIEF PLAN

- **Assessment**: Take a moment to assess each sector of your Grieving Wheel of Life. Where do you stand currently in each?
- **Goal Setting**: Once assessed, use your analytical brain to set manageable goals for each sector. Remember, these can be small, incremental steps.
- **Emotional Check-In**: Allow your intuitive, emotional side to weigh in. Do these goals resonate with how you're feeling? Are they aligned with your emotional needs right now?
- **Strategy**: Apply your whole-brain thinking to create actionable steps for each goal. Your analytical side will break down the 'how,' while your emotional side infuses each step with personal meaning.
- **Re-evaluation**: Life isn't static, especially during grief. Regularly reassess your Wheel and adjust your goals and strategies accordingly. Use members of your Board of Trust-eds to help.
- **Support Network**: Scheduled meetings with your Board of Trust-eds are ideal for sharing your re-evaluations and to.reshape your life plan. Their insight and feedback can provide additional whole-brain perspectives that you might not have considered.
- **Implementation**: Now, the most crucial step—take action. It could be as simple as taking a walk or joining a grief support group, or as complex as creating a financial

strategy for your changed circumstances. Even small acts can make a meaningful difference.

The idea here is not to master each aspect overnight but to create a balanced, whole-brain approach to navigating the labyrinth of grief and the unpredictable terrain of a life reshaped by loss. Even as you circumnavigate this disorienting landscape, take solace in the notion that your sorrow carries its own form of wisdom, and within your grief lies the potential for renewal and growth.

Harnessing the full spectrum of your brain's capabilities requires not just energy and focus, but also a dynamic approach, especially when navigating the stormy waters of life-altering loss. While it's true we're often categorized as either right-brained (creative) or left-brained (logical), the actuality is that our brain's brilliance lies in its ability to function as a multi-faceted orchestra, continuously collecting, sorting, and channeling information to various centers within itself. So why not make that a conscious endeavor, an intentional act?

Creating room for stillness and openness enables you to fully engage with whole-brain thinking. Yes, you might have a predisposition towards a specific learning style or way of interacting with your surroundings—established neuronal pathways that your brain gravitates to because, well, it's the path of least resistance. But here's the kicker: Your brain also loves novelty. When you shake up your thinking patterns by using novel approaches to solving a problem, you're not just stirring the pot; you're firing up neurons and stepping into the realm of neuroplasticity!

Take this as an invitation to break away from the familiar. Try using a technique known as a brain dump, then transition into creating a mind map*. Be the intellectual, the artist, the innovator, the home-life connoisseur. Lean into what you're naturally good at, but also stretch those mental muscles into territories where you haven't yet ventured.Whole-brain thinking not only makes you more versatile, but it also primes you for solving the unique set of challenges that come with life's most significant changes, such as the loss of a loved one. By embracing a whole-brain strategy, you're arming yourself with a comprehensive set of tools to navigate the complexities of moving forward with your life. Leverage your genius and expand it!

Your Board of Trust-eds is the perfect structure to actually see how this can work. Chances are there are several different personality types on your board, each one bringing a particular genius to you that will help you uncover options you might not otherwise see.

> "The biggest mistake I made concerning my financial assets was not consulting with a professional financial planner. I didn't trust them. Of course, what I didn't trust was my cynical version of them. After all, I had worked on Wall Street at the beginning of the Reagan era and I could see the direction we were headed in from the emerging culture of greed talk among the people I worked with. I felt a deep distrust for anyone connected with that world, and financial planners fell into that broad category even though I had never spoken to a certified financial planner. So, how do you go about finding someone who can work with you, or more importantly, who you can work with? I encourage you to find one—interview some and find one you like.
>
> Read their online reviews. Choose one and set an appointment. Bring some questions with you. Some of you reading this might think you don't have the assets to work with a financial planner. Don't be discouraged by this; there are services that can help you understand how to grow financial assets. Whatever your situation is, ideally you have found the person to help guide your financial well-being and they are a member of your Board of Trust-eds!"

17

FINANCIAL EMPOWERMENT

I can promise you, no matter what your finances are—easy street or struggling to pay the bills—you must have a financial strategy for yourself and for your family. My flimsy financial strategy didn't play out well as I had no one I trusted to discuss it with, so I held my cards close. My mistake was sharing my idea with someone I had just met! You see, I always knew real estate was a fantastic asset to have, so I decided to invest in real estate. Now this wouldn't have been a bad move if I wasn't in the clutches of grief and involved romantically with a sociopath. But as it turned out, I was. So dear ones, having the advice of a financial advisor on your Board of Trust-eds is a genius move. Even if you have a financial background, trust me, don't hold your own counsel when it comes to your finances. Not on this journey because there's a genuine chance for bad decisions. You really need to have this in place before another relationship enters your life. It's imperative for your financial security and safety.

First, you'll need to gather some information together before you even begin to talk to someone. You'll need to find out what your assets are and where they are. You'll need to assess your debts.

Answer questions like: What kind of future do you foresee for your children, for yourself, for your retirement? We're looking to empower your finances. To find a balance and create a budget that works for the lifestyle you desire, you need to begin now with the help of a professional.

I made big mistakes with my finances, grasping the money so tightly that it slipped through my hands. I didn't make investments that would sustain my children. I mistakenly did not put money aside for them, every month, every year. This was a big mistake. A mistake that cost peace of mind, even now. What was I thinking? I say this because I would like you to really contemplate this. What is it that you want for your children? For their future? Begin to plan it financially now. Are you getting survivors' benefits for them? Put some of that into a savings plan for them. Consult with the financial member of your board.

Do you need the survivors' benefits you're receiving for yourself to live on right now? To replace your love's income? To pay bills? I understand if that's the case. But maybe you could put 10% of that into a savings account for you. Call it your "rainy day" fund, but try to save some amount of money, no matter how small the amount might be, every month. Perhaps you can afford to do this on a weekly basis; if so, do it now.

There are a lot of extraneous things to consider when you lose your partner. One of them is do you need to go back into the work-force? Shortly after my husband passed, I had a friend telling me that I might be okay for a year or two but that I would need to go back to work. It set my mind reeling. How would I be able to take care of my children and go back to full-time work? In two years my kids would be in the throws of teenagehood. Yikes. This statement from my friend solidified my decision to go into business for myself. After all, I had the money to do that.

Part of your financial strategy is determining if you need to work for your financial security and what that looks like. Will you go back to an existing job? Do you need to figure out a career for yourself?

What does that look like? If you're going back to an existing job, what are your feelings about it? Do you need a career change? What kind of education or certification would that require? Think back to who you were before you met your partner. Does anything you wanted for yourself at that time resonate with you now?

18

MINDFULNESS AND NEUROSCIENCE

Where does this all fit into your life? As you might remember, I am a student and practitioner of Tibetan Buddhism. It's been almost 50 years since I started on that path. The path of taming and training your mind, examining your thoughts, contemplating your emotional reactions, looking at the duality of energies in your existence, both the wisdom side and the neurotic side. In the best of times, I could diffuse my reactionary responses and act with compassion. But this was the worst of times, my brain on grief had hijacked my mind. Yes, I could breathe into calming myself, calming the anxieties, the worries, the despair and, after my "affair" with Chapter Two had ended, the torment. Torment about the rash decisions I had made in those first two years, worry about my financial security as I approached senior citizenship.

I wrote earlier about the brain's efficiency and how our neural pathways create mental shortcuts. Shortcuts are habits, habitual patterns that create aspects of how we perceive and deal with the world, aspects of our personalities. Our childhood informs these habitual brain pathways, how we responded to what we were dealt.

These become our fallbacks when the brain senses the familiarity of an emotion that's arising because of what we're dealing with, what we've been emotionally stimulated by. Habitual patterns are based on hope and fear and remember, our amygdala is more susceptible to fear.

These shortcuts aren't always in our best interest when facing a traumatic experience like grieving the death of a significant person in our lives, a person whose death has altered our reality. Being able to calm your mind from spinning out is an excellent "tool" to have when you're facing a crisis. Meditation is about taming and training your mind by looking at your thoughts, and understanding the different "types" of thoughts that lead to strong emotions, anxiety, fear, energetic afflictions. It's the idea of riding a horse, does the rider have her seat or is the horse in charge? It's also about learning how to drive the vehicle, so to speak: learning the gears, learning how to steer, backup, backup using a camera, parallel park.

There's a second step and it's often overlooked because once we calm our fear center (our amygdala), our brain can override this step by its habitual tendencies, which are the brain's shortcuts, whether habitually hopeful or habitually fearful. When we bring our awareness to this function of our brain, we will have the presence of mind to engage consciously in whatever is in front of us, whatever we need to figure out. Learning about the brain's systems, about neuroscience, is looking under the hood. It's knowing where to pour in the washer fluid versus where the oil goes. It's knowing the basic systems and functionality, how to pop the hood, where the spare tire is. This is not getting a degree in auto mechanics or neuroscience. This is a simple understanding of the brain, how the brain and mind work together, and how we can learn to take our seat as the rider and navigate ourselves, our life, through this state of grief and loss.

Imagine you're driving a car and it has a manual transmission, so you need to shift gears by depressing the clutch and moving the gear stick manually. It's the same thing when you've quelled your mind through breathing or running or walking, meditation, prayer—

whatever it is you do to bring peace to your grief. As far as the stick-shift image goes, when you've depressed the clutch, the car is now in a neutral space. This is where you need to make a decision: do you put the car into another gear or let it idle in neutral, with the eventuality of the engine turning off when it runs out of gas? It takes energy to make the decision to engage the gears. As for your brain, it's using up a lot of its energy on your grief process. And because the brain loves efficiency, without you blinking an eye, it can revert to its shortcuts and this process, my dears, can lead you to make rash decisions, ones that might seem irrational to others and in hindsight, to yourself. The very next step, after you've calmed your emotional, fearful brain and without missing a heartbeat, is to put that stick shift into drive and use one of the exercises in this book to engage your boss brain, that CEO of your life, the higher power of your brain.

The practice of mindfulness and meditation *(see Appendix 6 for the Guide for Meditation Practice)* empowers the inner you, opens you to your intuition, connects you to your body and sensory awareness, and activates your frontal lobes. Understanding how the brain and mind work together adds rocket fuel to that empowerment. Through mindfulness, we can train our brain to take conscious action, to notice when we're falling into a habitual pattern that does not serve us well, and to work consciously to form a more productive shortcut for our brain. You surely know by now that our brain loves its shortcuts because it saves energy and time, so let's create neuronal pathways that lead to higher-level thinking!

Meditation and mindfulness allow openness to thoughts and experiences, being with ourselves, our inner and outer worlds with presence in a real-time moment. It's mostly your right hemisphere that's active here. When overwhelming thoughts and emotions come up, we have two choices: take the high road and be conscious about our engagement, or take the low road and follow a habitual pattern. Conscious action engages our PFC, whereas unconscious action leads to a limbic-system response. So what do we do if we're in the midst of an emotional outburst? This is when we can engage our left-brain hemisphere and find out the details of the feeling, the emotion. Where do you feel it in your body? Challenge it: is it logical? What are the facts? Are you being chased by a tiger right now? Both your right- and left-brain hemispheres are interactive, which now allows for more powerful problem solving by your PFC.

When we look at our thoughts in a non-judgmental way, we allow them to arise, to be, to dissolve, without following them down a rabbit hole. If feelings come up, allow them to arise, then consciously notice where they reside in your body. Don't deny those feelings that resurface again and again; it could be that they're stuck and need to be released. Breathe into the spots you feel stuck, the unresolved feelings that grief brings to us. Use this technique to lean into making friends with yourself and with your grief, something that is going to be your companion for the rest of your life. Something that will shift over time and not have as much control over you as it once did. Taking charge of how grief is affecting your brain and hijacking your mind can shorten that process while still honoring the loss you have suffered.

Grief is your story. How are you going to write it? It begins as a tragedy. It's a roller coaster with stomach-turning highs and lows. It completely takes over when you think you've put the worst behind you. When you realize it isn't just your person whom you've lost, there are secondary losses that are subtle and can trigger you when you least expect it.

19

ACCEPTING GRIEF AS A
LIFELONG PROCESS

Grief is not a linear path; in fact, the path of grief is arduous. There are rocky parts and ledges with glorious views. There are days of isolation when you won't want to leave your house, and other days when you need that next adventure and your community. There will be days between these two extremes also. Days of reflection, of the need to organize and get on with life. It's a wild ride. You can take comfort in the fact that this is how it is. Grief is a dual process.[1] The idea here is that coping with loss involves a complex balancing act between two different types of stressors: loss-oriented and restoration-oriented. In simpler terms, loss-oriented stressors focus on the grief itself—the emotional pain, yearning, and other feelings directly related to the loss. These are the aspects that many people traditionally associate with mourning, like crying, looking at old photos, or visiting the grave of the loved one.

Restoration-oriented stressors, on the other hand, are more about the secondary changes or adjustments that one has to make because of the loss. This can include taking on new roles that the deceased used to fill, adjusting to a financial change, or even just learning how to spend your time now that the person is no longer part of your daily life. These tasks are more "practical" in nature but are also emotionally draining in their own way.

You can't just focus on one and ignore the other; it's not healthy to solely dwell on your emotional pain, nor is it advisable to keep yourself too busy to confront your feelings. The balance doesn't have to be 50-50, and it's likely to shift from day to day or even hour to hour. But the idea is that you allow yourself the space to feel your loss while also giving yourself permission to continue living and changing.

I think it helps to understand that there are days when you will "take a break" from grief automatically. Not something you plan on a calendar, but something your brain and body dance between. So, when we say grief is a dual process, it's a recognition of this intricate dance between the heart and the mind, the past and the present, and even sorrow and renewal.

There's going to be a struggle. A push/pull struggle. We don't want what happened (the death of our love) to be the deciding factor in our state of being, so there's a sense of pushing it away, far away from our present moment. A distancing from the downright pain and emotional distress that engulfs our minds and spirit. Or we pull our grief into a warm cocoon of our very own, licking our wounds. Somehow there's an ounce of comfort in being that way. I've often felt some solace here, a feeling of being close to the one(s) I've lost to death. This is not, however, the place to settle, to make a nest or home no matter your current situation (a mom with young kids or teenagers; an empty nester) or how many years it's been since you've been treading on this path. It's a place to acknowledge but not to get lost or stuck in.

Yes, there will come the time when you'll realize that accepting your grief—accepting that you're bound to mourn this loss forever—is a compassionate step to take for yourself. This compassionate expression is composed of gentleness towards yourself and faith that you can make decisions that aren't reactively based on "because of" but rather on a decisive direction. Decisions based on counsel, not on flight. You can be precise and clear because your mind understands how fear is set off in your brain and how you can make whole brain-based decisions that help you grow within your grief. You can see a natural next step forward, one when clarity reigns and precision leads.

We don't want to experience how bad things are so our coping mechanism is not to deal with the complexity of our grief. We will just deal with the tasks of our life one day at a time. If you have children this is "easy" to do. We put our children first and put dealing with our grief on the back burner. We attempt to normalize our children's lives. We keep their routines intact, their playdates, and their schooling. We enroll them in bereavement groups, seek school counseling, and talk with their pediatricians. We notice how each one of them may experience and deal with their grief and the loss of a parent in totally different ways. Our concern focuses on them. A distraction from looking at our grief. "I'm strong, I'm resilient. This is my job, I have to raise these kids." We deal with our kids' emotions, emergency after emergency, one thing at a time with no time to allow space for exploring our own grief. We put what we're going through to the side, sheltering our children's loss by keeping normalcy in their lives.

Where does this get you? From my own experience, it becomes more complicated as the years go on and your children grow into adults. When do you finally have time to process and deal with this shocking turn your life took?

Providing yourself with the space to look at and understand grief and your unique grief journey is essential to being able to embrace your life, rise from what grief has thrown at you, and find a direction beyond fear and not based on wishful thinking. Your life can blossom based on a foundation of trusting your next step, a bold next step. My wish for you is that the information in this book will inspire your growth and well-being as you navigate your journey with grief.

EPILOGUE

At the time of this writing, I have had 28 years to look back on and mourn over all the things he missed. Birthdays, graduations, anniversaries, holidays and just plain old ordinary days—over 10,000 of them. Twenty-eight years of living through Labor Days. It wasn't easy to write about "my story." Sometimes it felt like descending into the depths of what feels like a cave to me. My cave of "His Death." You'll have your cave, too. Maybe it'll take on another name for you. Cave works for me. In this cave, I am alone with David's death. The day that led up to it, the day of it, the next day and next day, and weeks and months, and how the years turned into 28 of them. David's death cave is a place where I can find solace. It's a place I can go to in my mind. It's a place where I can talk to him, write to him, and listen to him whispering, "You've done well. You're my Queen. I'm sorry, it was an accident."

28 years. My grief journey was complicated by the choices I made and their outcomes. That fateful Chapter 2 relationship that created more loss and more grief. That positioned me to understand the different experiences people go through that result in a loss and

cause us to grieve. I understand feeling overwhelmed by ordinary daily existence and how hard it is to take small, bold, courageous steps towards moving forward with life—all while processing loss and grief.

Everyone's grief journey has a different duration. I spent the first ten of these 28 years circling in the labyrinth of my grief. Not understanding how the brain on grief and loss can sabotage the effect of mindfulness meditations, of my meditation practice. Meditation can calm the mind and open space for spiritual growth; as such, it can offer temporary soothing and a false security that we've got our grief, that I had my grief, "under control." After all, I could calm my mind and bring balance to my overwhelming emotional state.

There came a point when neuroscience and brain research caught my curiosity. I spent the next ten years reading up and doing research on what I perceived as the interconnection of the brain and the mind. It was during that time I met and studied with Shonté Jovan Taylor.

In the last eight years since my husband's death, I've been researching and writing this book with the inspiration to bring an understanding of grief's effect on the brain and how that translates into hijacking the mind and sabotaging the idea that mindfulness meditation alone can assuage grief and loss. I combine a unique perspective in working with grief by entwining my knowledge of meditation (working with the mind) with my training as a certified neuroscience coach (understanding the brain).

My research for this book has led me to explore the many intersections of our brain, our emotions and our consciousness, all of which is fodder for another book, or perhaps two.

If you'd like to learn more about my work and the workshops I offer, please visit **www.thewidowdoula.com**

COMING IN 2025 AND BEYOND:

- *Portrait Of A Wakeful Mind &*
- *The Truth of Impermanence: Beyond Hope & Fear*

ACKNOWLEDGMENTS

Writing this book has been a profound experience and dive into the depths of understanding my grief. I want to express my gratitude and thanks to the many people who have been my guides through this process.

To my dear friends, Lori Einhorn, Andrea Doukas and Barbara Stewart for reading it in its early stages and offering their support and insights.

To my editor, Mimi Rich, for her kindness and wisdom. To my publisher, Sierra Melcher for her patience, tough love, and care throughout the birthing of this book.

To the generous community of Red Thread Publishing staff and authors.

To the many women who have supported my journey: Liza Rowe, Patrice Berg, Joanne O'Brien, K.C. Baker, Bernadette Pleasant, Anastazja Gajkowska, Piret Rass, Carol Cabbiness, and Kim Pearlstein. I have grown wise through knowing you.

To Shonté Jovan Taylor, I offer a deep bow of appreciation. The knowledge you share about our brain gave me the understanding I needed to proceed.

To my family, my mom and dad, Dolly and Tony, who were lifelines during the dark days of my life. To my sister, Pam; and my brothers, Tom, Steven and Marc, for their continuous love and support. To my cousin, Judy Feury; our conversations uplift me.

To Robert Fierman, my dearest friend and love, whose friendship, caring, and protection throughout the years has brought a beautiful brilliance to my life.

And to you, dear reader, thank you for reading this book.

xo

THANK YOU

If you have enjoyed or found value in this book, please take a moment to leave an honest and brief review on Amazon (here is the direct link **amzn.to/3ROie9b**) or <u>Goodreads</u>. Your reviews help prospective readers decide if this is right for them & it is the greatest kindness you can offer the author.

Thank you in advance.

ABOUT THE AUTHOR

Therese Marchitelli is a neuro-grief & loss coach and trainer, known as The Widow Doula. Her services provide people who are grieving a loss and feel overwhelmed by their ordinary daily existence the support and guidance to take small, bold, courageous steps to move forward with their lives while understanding and processing their losses and grief.

Therese uses her experience as a meditation instructor, student, and practitioner in the Tibetan Buddhist tradition for 48 years synergistically with her study and training in neuro-grief and loss to bring a unique understanding of grief's effect on the brain. Through coaching and training, she does all of this with love, protection, and clarity.

www.thewidowdoula.com

Photo by Kris Giacobbe Photography

ABOUT THE PUBLISHER

WRITE.PUBLISH.IMPACT.
www.RedThreadBooks.com

Red Thread Publishing is an all-female publishing company on a mission to support 10,000 women to become successful published authorpreneurs & thought leaders.

To work with us or connect regarding any of our growing library of books email us at **info@redthreadbooks.com.**

To learn more bout us visit our website **www.redthreadbooks.com.**

Follow us & join the community.

f facebook.com/redthreadpublishing

instagram.com/redthreadbooks

APPENDIX

1. FIGHT, FLIGHT, FREEZE, FAWN

The "fight, flight, freeze, and fawn" responses are part of our biological reaction to stress or danger. Each response serves a purpose and can be effective depending on the situation. They can also manifest in complex ways when dealing with emotional or psychological stress.

Here's a brief description of each:

Fight

- **Activation:** Body and mind prepare to confront the threat directly
- **Physiological response:** Release of adrenaline, increased heart rate, sharpening of senses
- **Behavioral traits:** Aggressiveness, confrontation, problem-solving under pressure

Flight

- **Activation**: Body and mind prepare to evade or escape the threat
- **Physiological response**: Similar to the fight response—adrenaline release, increased heart rate
- **Behavioral traits**: Quick decision-making aimed at evasion, running away, or avoiding the situation

Freeze

- **Activation**: Body and mind halt all non-essential actions to become less noticeable or to evaluate the situation
- **Physiological response**: Decreased heart rate, shallow breathing, enhanced perception
- **Behavioral traits**: Inaction, minimal movement, silent observation, waiting for an opportune moment

Fawn

- **Activation**: Body and mind prepare to defuse the threat by appeasing or pleasing the aggressor
- **Physiological response**: Lowered guard, submissive body language, focus on the needs of the aggressor
- **Behavioral traits**: People-pleasing, appeasement, submission, sacrificing own needs for safety

2. GRIEF TRIGGERS

For someone who has lost their person, a variety of experiences, memories, and situations can serve as triggers for grief. This is also true for other life-changing losses that cause grief. These triggers can sometimes be unexpected and may arise at any time—even years after the loss.

Here are some of the common ones:

Dates and anniversaries:

- Birthdays
- Death anniversaries
- Anniversaries
- Holidays: winter holidays, Thanksgiving, cultural celebrations or other family-centered celebrations

Places and locations:

- Visiting a place significant to the relationship
- Seeing the deceased's favorite spots or places where memories were created
- Visiting the grave or memorial site

Objects and mementos:

- Photographs of the deceased or the times spent together
- Keepsakes, gifts, or letters from the deceased
- Clothing or other belongings of the deceased

Sounds and music:

- Hearing a song that holds emotional significance
- Sounds that are reminiscent of the deceased (e.g., their laughter, a specific tune they loved)
- Voice recordings or videos that include the deceased

Scents and tastes:

- Smelling a fragrance associated with the deceased (e.g., their perfume or cologne)

- Cooking or tasting foods that were favorites or shared meals

Social interactions:

- Seeing someone who closely resembles the deceased
- Hearing someone with a similar name or voice
- Encounters with mutual friends or family members who also knew the deceased

Life milestones:

- Significant events where the absence of the deceased is strongly felt (e.g., graduations, weddings, the birth of a child)
- Achieving something that you wish you could share with the deceased (e.g., a promotion, retirement)

Media:

- Watching a movie or reading a book that was a favorite or is thematically related to the deceased
- News or social media updates related to the cause of death (e.g., cancer research, car safety)

Emotional states:

- Experiencing a moment of joy, success, or love and wanting to share it with the deceased
- Feeling lonely or vulnerable, and missing the support of the deceased

Changes in life circumstances:

- Entering into a new relationship or stage of life where the deceased's absence is felt acutely
- Dealing with other losses or stressors that compound the original grief

Each person's experience of grief is unique, and what serves as a trigger for one person may not have the same effect on another. These triggers may also change over time as you navigate the complexities of your grief.

3. LIFE EVENTS THAT CAN CAUSE US TO GRIEVE

Grief not only happens because of the death of a person; people grieve about a wide range of events, and what triggers grief is a highly individual experience. Understanding the events that we might grieve can be helpful for both individuals going through the experience and those offering support.

Here are some examples of life events and situations that people commonly grieve:

Death and loss:

- Death of a loved one (e.g., parent, spouse, child, close friend or relative, pet)
- Death of a person you have a complicated relationship with
- Miscarriage or stillbirth
- Death of a friend or colleague
- Loss of a significant relationship through separation or divorce

Health:

- Personal diagnosis of a serious or chronic illness

- Illness of a family member or close friend
- Injury or disability affecting quality of life

Life changes:

- Retirement or job loss
- Moving to a new location, leaving behind friends/family
- Children leaving home (empty-nest syndrome)

Identity and self-image:

- Experiencing a significant life failure (e.g., failed business, academic failure)
- Aging and confronting mortality
- Loss of physical abilities or attractiveness
- Experiencing trauma or assault

Social and cultural factors:

- Isolation from community or social circles
- Discrimination or prejudice based on race, gender, sexual orientation, etc.
- Cultural or religious reasons, such as loss of faith or community

Unexpected life events:

- Natural disasters causing loss of home or livelihood
- Sudden financial hardships
- Legal problems leading to stress or loss of freedom

Relationships:

- Betrayal or breach of trust within a relationship

- Loss of social status or reputation
- Conflict within family or friend groups that leads to emotional distress

Other:

- Global events causing widespread anxiety (e.g., pandemics, wars)
- Celebrations that bring up memories of lost loved ones (e.g., holidays, birthdays)
- Anniversaries of past losses or traumas

4. SAMPLE CONTRACT TEMPLATE FOR YOUR BOARD OF TRUST-EDS:

The concept of a "Board of Trust-eds" is an innovative and compassionate way to provide a structured support system for someone who is going through the difficult process of grieving the death of their spouse or life partner. This formal "contract" can help solidify the commitments and expectations of everyone involved.

Board of Trust-eds Commitment Contract for Grief Support

Introduction

This contract is to establish the roles, responsibilities, and expectations of board members participating in the "Board of Trust-eds," created to support [Grieving Individual's Name] ("Grieving Individual") who has recently lost a spouse or life partner.

Purpose:

The purpose of this board is to offer a specialized support structure around the Grieving Individual, with each board member serving a unique role that equates to a facet of life as identified in the "Wheel of Life" by life coaches.

Contract Duration:

This contract will remain active from [Starting Date] through [End Date], covering the initial critical year following the loss.

Board Member Roles:

Identify the role that you are committing to, such as emotional support, financial guidance, spiritual counseling, well-being, etc.

Role: _____

Meetings:

- **Weekly Meetings:** Board members commit to attend a weekly meeting with the Grieving Individual for the first month following the loss.
- **Monthly Meetings:** After the first month, board members will attend meetings once a month for the remainder of the year.
- **Special Sessions:** Board members may be called for additional meetings or one-on-one sessions as the need arises.

Commitments:

- **Confidentiality:** To maintain a private and confidential environment where the Grieving Individual can freely express their emotions and concerns.
- **Timeliness:** To be punctual for all scheduled meetings and appointments.
- **Compassion:** To provide non-judgmental and empathic support.
- **Professional Guidance:** To offer specialized advice and support related to your role on the board.

- **Consistency:** To be consistently present and available, to the best of your ability, for the Grieving Individual throughout the duration of this contract.
- **Boundaries:** To be aware of and maintain appropriate professional and personal boundaries.

Acknowledgement:

By signing below, I acknowledge and agree to uphold the commitments outlined in this contract to the best of my ability.

Board Member's Name: _____

Board Member's Signature: _____

Date: _____

This contract can be tailored to fit the specific needs and circumstances of your Board and the individual you're supporting. It is recommended to consult with legal advisors for a more formalized agreement.

5. MIND MAPPING

Making a mind map is like creating a visual playground for your ideas. It's a great way to get a bird's-eye view of a topic or just to organize your thoughts in a creative way .

Here's how you can do it:

- **Start with a central idea:** Grab a blank piece of paper and a pen. Write down the central topic or idea smack-dab in the middle. Draw a circle around it or make it stand out somehow.
- **Branch out:** From the central idea, draw lines, or "branches," outward. At the end of each line, jot down a

related sub-topic or idea. These are like the big subheadings under your main title.

- **Sub-branches**: Now, for each of those first-level ideas, draw smaller lines branching out. Here, you can list even more specific details, examples, or related ideas/concepts. You can get as detailed as you want!
- **Get creative**: This is where you can let your artistic side shine. Use colors, icons, or doodles to help differentiate between ideas or show connections. Different line styles can also represent different types of relationships.
- **Connect ideas**: Found something that links back to another branch? Draw a line between them or somehow indicate that these ideas are connected. This helps you see relationships you might not have spotted otherwise.
- **Review and refine**: Once you've got your basic map, take a step back. Anything missing? Anything you could connect in a new way? Go ahead and add it in.
- **Use it**: Your mind map is not just a pretty picture; it's a tool. Use it to plan out your Board of Trust-eds, a life plan, brainstorm a project, or get a grip on complex information.
- **Iterate**: As you work on whatever you're using the mind map for, you may find that you need to add or adjust stuff. Go for it! A mind map is a living, breathing thing.

6. MEDITATION PRACTICE

Choose a quiet place. Sit cross-legged on a meditation cushion or a straight-backed chair with your feet flat on the floor.

Your back should be straight and your posture upright. If sitting on a chair, don't lean back. Place your hands palms down on your thighs. With your eyes open, let your gaze rest comfortably as you look slightly downward about six feet in front of you.

Place your attention lightly on your out-breath. Take a moment to connect with your breath. Breathe at your own pace and take a few moments to feel the rhythm of your breathing as it slows down and relaxes into the state of your body being at rest.

Be with each breath as the air goes out through your mouth and nostrils and dissolves into the space around you. At the end of each out-breath, simply rest with your in-breath until the next breath goes out.When a thought comes up, label it "thinking" and return to following your breath as it goes out. Thoughts are neither good nor bad; they just are. This is also true of any sensations you might feel, sounds you might hear, etc. You are not isolating yourself from your environment; you have an awareness of it but are not indulging in distractions.

If you're just beginning a meditation practice, try meditating for ten minutes in the morning. When you feel settled in the benefits of meditation, increase it to ten minutes in the morning and ten in the evening. Ideally, you could aim for twenty minutes in both the morning and the evening. Then, when you've finished with your meditation session, let the calmness and mindfulness you've gained be your guide for the day.

GLOSSARY OF TERMS USED

BEREAVEMENT, GRIEF, AND MOURNING

I'm a social scientist by nature; it's also what I have a degree in. I'm intrigued by language and how we use it to communicate and describe what we're experiencing. We all have a unique journey with grief, though there are shared experiences in that they include our emotions, physical health, spiritual leanings, and psychology.

In my study of grief and loss, and again, being a social scientist who wants to understand more about the common threads that are woven between us on this journey, I liked the clarification of and distinction among the terms bereavement, grief, and mourning used by M. Katherine Shear, MD in an article she wrote on complicated grief*. Therefore, I have used them in defining my experiences throughout this book.

Bereavement encompasses grief and loss. According to the Merriam-Webster dictionary, bereavement is "the state or fact of being bereaved or deprived of something or someone; the experience of having lost someone." Dr. Shear states "bereavement refers to the experience of having lost someone close."

Although bereavement is associated with losing someone through their death, it can also be triggered by other losses like a divorce or health issues.

While bereavement is facing the reality of the loss, **grief** is the response to it. Grief is an internal process. It's all the emotional ups and downs we experience after a loss. Grief hurts, psychologically and physically. Grieving the death of a loved one has no end to it. Depending upon our connection to the deceased person, we can grieve their loss for as long as we live.

Mourning takes on an external aspect. It is how we become through our grief journey. It is how we face the world without our loved one. It is the outward expression of our grief and how others see us. Mourning is how we integrate our grief into our life and how we move forward while grieving.

Brain Dump

A brain dump is basically when you take all the thoughts, ideas, or information swirling around in your head and just unload it onto paper, a computer, or whatever medium works for you. It's like emptying out your mental "junk drawer" so you can see what you've got, sort it out, and make sense of it all. People often do brain dumps to declutter their mind, plan a project, or just to get a better handle on what they're thinking or feeling. It's a useful way to free up some mental space!

Mind Map

A mind map is a way to visually organize your thoughts, ideas, or even tasks. You put your central topic or concept in the middle, and then you draw branches out to related ideas, topics, or subtopics. It's like a tree for your thoughts that are related to the specific topic you're working on. You can use colors, icons, and whatever else helps you get a better picture of your idea. It's helpful for brainstorming, or planning out projects. Unlike a brain dump, which is more like a mental free-for-all, a mind map gives structure to your thoughts.

*See Bibliograpy

RESOURCES

In the spirit of nurturing the communities that have formed to serve people who are grieving, here are some you might want to check out.

What's Your Grief – https://whatsyourgrief.com What's Your Grief is a fantastic resource for all types of loss. It was founded by two mental health professionals who had their own journey with grief. Check out their recently published book, *What's Your Grief, Lists to Help You Through Any Loss.*

Good Grief – https://good-grief.org Good Grief is centered around providing support for children who have lost a parent, sibling, or caregiver.

Soaring Spirits International – https://soaringspirits.org Soaring Spirits' goal is to connect widowed people with one another. And they do this well and through a number of innovative programs — Camp Widow, regional groups, widow penpals.

Modern Loss – https://modernloss.com One of my favorites! Modern Loss uses humor, albeit somewhat dark, to point a finger at the disconnection a grieving person perceives from the "outside world". They are funny and poignant with their education about processing grief.

Modern Widows Club – https://modernwidowsclub.org An excellent place to begin if you're newly widowed. Caroline Moore, the founder, has brilliant insights about navigating grief. If you're lucky, there's a local group in your area. If not, there are many resources and ways to connect online. Including an annual conference and clubs you can join — check out the Travel Club!!

Center For Loss – This organization is led by death educator and grief counselor Dr. Alan Wolfelt. They support people who are grieving as well as offer resources to grief work professionals.

Covid Grief Network – https://covidgriefnetwork.org was established to support and serve young adults who have lost someone through the Covid-19 Virus.

reimagine – https://letsreimagine.org reimagine (*sic*) takes loss and grief and channels that energy into meaningful action. They host community-driven events around the world, bringing creativity, connection and conversation to life's challenges and reimagining how we can embrace and move through hard times.

GRIEF.COM – https://grief.com was founded by David Kessler, who is an author and expert on grief and loss. There are many resources, more books, and information on their website.

Hope For Widows Foundation – https://hopeforwidows.org offers support to women who have lost their life partner. Grounded in experience and community, this site is a gem.

BIBLIOGRAPHY

Anderson, Susan, *Suffering the Death of a Loved One*. Healing Abandonment, 2006.

Burdette, Cindy. *How a Child's Developmental Stage Impacts Their Grief*. Hospice of the Panhandle.

Devine, Megan. *It's OK That You're Not OK*. Boulder: Sounds True. 2017.

Dora, Kenneth, J. *Grief is a Journey: Finding Your Way Through Loss*. New York: Atria. 2016.

Frankl, Viktor. *Man's Search For Meaning*. New York: Touchstone, 1984.

Gawande, Atul. *The Checklist Manifesto*. New York: Picador, 2009.

Greenspan, Miriam. *Healing Through The Dark Emotions*. Boston: Shambhala Publications, 2003.

Halifax, Joan. *Standing At The Edge*. New York: Flatiron Books, 2018.

Hanson, Rick. *Buddha's Brain*. Oakland: New Harbinger Publications, 2009.

Holing, Dorothy. *The Anatomy of Grief*. New Haven: Yale University Press, 2020.

James, John, and Russell Friedman. When Children Grieve. New York: Harper Collins, 2004.

Langshur, Eric, and Nate Klemp. Start Here. New York: North Way Star, 2016.

Leaf, Caroline. Cleaning Up Your Mental Mess. Grand Rapids: Baker Books, 2021.

Lews, C.S. *A Grief Observed*. New York: Harper One, 1994.

Melcher, Sierra. *Date Yourself*. Red Thread Publishing, 2022.

O'Conner, Mary-Frances. *The Grieving Brain*. New York: Harper One, 2022.

Shulman, Lisa M. *Before & After Loss*. Baltimore: John Hopkins University Press, 2018.

Shear, M. Katherine. *"Grief and Mourning Gone Awry: Pathway and Course of Complicated Grief."* Dialogues in Neuroscience: National Library of Medicine, 2012.

Shear, M. Katherine. *"Complicated Grief And Related Bereavement Issues."* Dialogues in Neuroscience: National Library of Medicine, 2011.

Shonté Jovan Taylor, *OptiMind Institute,* www.shontejtaylor.com

Thich Nhat Hanh, *Living Buddha, Living Christ*. New York: Riverhead Books, 1995.

Van Der Kolk, Besell. *The Body Keeps the Score*. New York: Viking. 2014.

Wilson, John. *The Plain Guide to Grief*. 2020.

Wortman, Camille B. *"Post Traumatic Growth: Progress & Problems."* State University of New York at Stony Brook: Department of Psychology, 2004.

Notes

PROLOGUE

1. "How To Write" — Anne Waldman, *Paris Review, 1968*

UNDERSTANDING OUR BRAIN ON GRIEF

1. Hebb's axiom is a foundational principle in neuroscience, originally proposed by psychologist Donald Hebb in 1949. The axiom is often summarized by the phrase, "Cells that fire together, wire together." What this means is that when two neurons are activated simultaneously, the strength of the synaptic connection between them increases. Simply put, experiences that cause certain patterns of neuronal activity lead to changes in the brain's wiring, making it more likely that those neurons will fire together in the future.

7. RITUALS

1. "Amygdala hijack" is term coined by Daniel Goleman, author of *Emotional Intelligence: Why It Can Matter More Than IQ.*

14. CREATING A LIFE PLAN,

1. *Date Yourself* by Sierra Melcher offers in-depth work and a practical guide for self-discovery.

19. ACCEPTING GRIEF AS A LIFELONG PROCESS

1. The concept of grief as a dual process was introduced by Margaret Stroebe and Henk Schut (*Death Studies*, 1999) through their work "The Dual Process Model of Coping with Bereavement: A Decade On."